SpringerBriefs in Computer Science

Series Editors

Stan Zdonik
Peng Ning
Shashi Shekhar
Jonathan Katz
Xindong Wu
Lakhmi C. Jain
David Padua
Xuemin Shen
Borko Furht
V. S. Subrahmanian
Martial Hebert
Katsushi Ikeuchi
Bruno Siciliano

For further volumes:
http://www.springer.com/series/10028

Flávia C. Delicato · Paulo F. Pires
Thais Batista

Middleware Solutions
for the Internet of Things

Springer

Flávia C. Delicato
Department of Computer Science
Federal University of Rio de Janeiro
Rio de Janeiro
RJ
Brazil

Thais Batista
Department of Computer Science
Federal University of Rio Grande
    do Norte
Natal
RN
Brazil

Paulo F. Pires
Department of Computer Science
Federal University of Rio de Janeiro
Rio de Janeiro
RJ
Brazil

ISSN 2191-5768   ISSN 2191-5776   (electronic)
ISBN 978-1-4471-5480-8   ISBN 978-1-4471-5481-5   (eBook)
DOI 10.1007/978-1-4471-5481-5
Springer London Heidelberg New York Dordrecht

Library of Congress Control Number: 2013945293

Printed on acid-free paper

Springer is part of Springer Science+Business Media (www.springer.com)

Preface

The *Internet of Things (IoT)* is a step forward in the well-known widespread Internet revolution. It consists of a world of physical objects embedded with sensors and actuators linked by wireless networks which communicate using the Internet, shaping a network of smart objects, with processing power and able to capture environmental variables, and to react to external stimuli. Such objects are connected and can be controlled over the Internet, enabling a myriad of novel applications. The IoT is one of the key technologies to enable the creation of cyber physical systems and realize the vision of Smart Cities. Several recent technological advances enabled the emergence of IoT such as nanotechnology, sensor networks, mobile communication, and ubiquitous computing. However, there are still a set of challenges to be addressed, mainly related to the development of IoT applications dealing with the heterogeneity arising from the diversity of hardware, sensors and actuators, and wireless technologies inherent to such environments.

Inspired in the IoT idea, a new application development paradigm has recently emerged, the *Web of Things (WoT)*, that uses Web technologies in the development of applications composed of smart objects that can be viewed and used in the same way as any other Web resource. The realization of the WoT paradigm requires that the World Wide Web, as we know, be extended so that real-world objects and embedded devices can be seamlessly incorporated into it. This extension is obtained by using the HTTP protocol and REST principles for creating RESTful APIs that allow Smart Objects to become Web resources. Furthermore, through the support, for instance, of middleware platforms, services may be provided on top of the resources connected to the Web so as to facilitate the fast combination of features to create multiple value-added applications, the so-called *physical mashups*.

Within the context of Web-enabled smart objects, the current form of integrating resources that are not natively HTTP compliant has several limitations and alternative architectures need to be proposed and evaluated. Moreover, in spite of the fast "populating" of WoT, it is necessary to develop a more standardized and scalable approach to integrate Smart Objects in the Web. Such approach must address multilevel integration issues. In the lower level, it is necessary to seamlessly integrate a myriad of heterogeneous physical devices with each other. At an intermediate level, in order to provide value-added services on top of the simple sensing service provided by the devices, it is necessary to easily integrate sensing data with Internet available functionality, ranging from simple data processing functions such as data aggregation to more complex Web applications. At the higher level, a standardized programming model can provide the ultimate integration level, delivering programming elements specifically tailored to transparently assemble and transform information from sensing devices without demanding any specific knowledge from the developer regarding the specificities of physical devices and networking environment.

The *SmartSensor infrastructure* is an example of the recent research initiatives aimed at addressing the aforementioned issues, which is based on current standardization efforts for enabling WoT. This infrastructure was developed to manage a specific type of physical devices, those organized to shape a Wireless Sensor Networks (WSN), where sensors work collaboratively, extracting environmental data, and transmitting it to one or more exit points of the network, to be analyzed and further processed. Such WSNs are useful for a wide range of application domains and their usage has grown enormously in the last decade. Therefore, in the SmartSensor infrastructure, sensor generated data are considered as a primordial resource to be shared in the Web. In addition, SmartSensor considers all levels of integration previously mentioned. SmartSensor provides: (i) integration of distinct WSNs, i.e., consisting of sensor nodes that adopt different technologies, hardware, and/or software; (ii) integration of WSN sensing data and functionality with other Web applications; and (iii) integration of WSN functionalities within a programming model that abstract the specificities of the WSN environment.

This book focuses on describing SmartSensor and how to develop an application for IoT/WoT using such an infrastructure. A parking lot application is adopted to illustrate the use of the SmartSensor infrastructure as an enabler of the smart city concept. The choosing of such a type of application is due to the increasing parking problems in big cities and also in mass events such as the Olympics, for instance. Although SmartSensor can be considered as a middleware for IoT, in its current version, it only provides communication and integration services as well as a programming model to develop applications on top of the WSN infrastructure. In the direction of providing a more broad view to the reader, we also describe the requirements that a full functional middleware for IoT should meet and present an overview of the state-of-the-art in IoT middleware.

This book should be of particular interest for researchers, students, professional developers who are interested in research trends related to IoT/WoT and who would like to have a broad understanding of IoT, and of how to develop IoT applications.

Rio de Janeiro, May 2013   Flávia C. Delicato
                                                                          Paulo F. Pires
Natal   Thais Batista

Acknowledgments

We would like to acknowledge all those who contributed for our work in the several subjects related to this Book. Special thanks to Jesús Martín Talavera Portocarrero, José Renato da Silva Júnior, Fabrício Firmino de Faria, and Henrique Romano Correia for their valuable support in developing SmartSensor.

We would like to thank the National Education and Research Network (RNP) for partially supporting this work, as the idea of this book grew out when the authors were involved in a project about Smart Cities supported by RNP.

Contents

Chapter 1
Introduction

Abstract The Internet of Things (IoT) is a step forward in the well-known wide-spread Internet revolution. It consists in a world of physical objects embedded with sensors and actuators linked by wireless networks and communicating using the Internet, shaping a network of smart objects, with processing power and able to capture environmental variables and to react to external stimuli. Such objects are connected and can be controlled over the Internet, enabling a myriad of novel applications. IoT is one of the key technologies to enable the creation of cyber physical systems and realize the vision of new IT application domains such as Smart Cities. Several recent technological advances enabled the emergence of IoT such as nanotechnology, wireless sensor networks, mobile communication, and ubiquitous computing. However, there is still a set of challenges to be addressed in order to fully realize the IoT paradigm, mainly related to the development of IoT applications dealing with the heterogeneity arising from the diversity of hardware, sensors and actuators, and wireless technologies inherent to such an environment.

Keywords Internet of Things (IoT) · Web of Things (WoT) · Smart objects · Smart-Sensor · Middleware · Applications for IoT

1.1 Motivation

The advances on electronic devices, communications, RFID technology and the explosive growth of the World Wide Web (WWW) have contributed to drive the development of the Internet of Things (IoT) paradigm [1, 2, 4, 11]. IoT enables the connection of the virtual and physical worlds, where physical objects, the so-called *smart objects* [6], are connected to the Internet and can be remotely controlled by users and even communicate with each other. IoT extends the traditional interaction between human and machines provided by the Internet to a new dimension, human-to-thing (H2T) and thing-to-thing (T2T) communications. As reported by the IoT

F. C. Delicato et al., *Middleware Solutions for the Internet of Things*,
SpringerBriefs in Computer Science, DOI: 10.1007/978-1-4471-5481-5_1,
© The Author(s) 2013

European Research Cluster group, the IoT applications can be applied to multiple domains, including: telecommunications, medical technology, healthcare, environment monitoring, agriculture and breeding, oil and gas, food traceability, intelligent buildings, safety, security and privacy and many more [4]. Considering the significance and high potential, governments, research institutes, industries and academics have paid great attention to IoT and its application in the past few years. IoT is included by the US National Intelligence Council (NIC) in the list of six "Disruptive Civil Technologies" with potential impacts on US national power [8]. NIC foresees that "by 2025 Internet nodes may reside in everyday things—food packages, furniture, paper documents, and more". Besides that, the US National Science Foundation (NSF) has identified IoT as a key area of research [8], and IBM proposed Smarter Planet as an industry implementation of IoT. Even though there are numerous projects and developments concerning certain aspects of the IoT, it is still in infancy and many research efforts need to be done to fully accomplish its potential.

Inspired on the IoT idea, a new application development paradigm has recently emerged, the so-called *Web of Things (WoT)*, which uses Web technologies in the development of applications composed of smart objects that can be viewed and used in the same way as any other Web resource. The realization of the WoT paradigm requires that the World Wide Web, as we know, be extended so that real-world objects and embedded devices can be seamlessly incorporated into it. This extension is obtained by using the Hypertext Transfer Protocol (HTTP)and the Representational State Transfer (REST) [5] principles for creating RESTful APIs that allow smart objects to become Web resources. The REST emphasis on resources that are addressed using URIs is described by the *Resource-Oriented Architecture* (ROA) [10]. Furthermore, through the support, for instance, of middleware platforms, services may be provided on top of the resources connected to the Web so as to facilitate the fast combination of features to create multiple value-added applications, the so-called *physical mashups* [3, 7]. Within the context of Web-enabled smart objects, the current form of integrating resources that are not natively HTTP compliant has several limitations [7] and alternative architectures need to be proposed and evaluated. Moreover, in spite of the fast "populating" of WoT, it is necessary to develop a more standardized and scalable approach to integrate smart objects in the Web. Such an approach must address multilevel integration issues. At the lower level, it is necessary to seamlessly integrate a myriad of heterogeneous physical devices with each other. At the intermediate level, in order to provide value-added services on top of the simple sensing service provided by the devices, it is necessary to easily integrate sensing data with Internet available functionality, ranging from simple data processing functions, such as data aggregation, to more complex Web applications. At the higher level, a standardized programming model can provide the ultimate integration level, delivering programming elements specifically tailored to transparently assemble and transform information from sensing devices, without demanding any specific knowledge from the developer regarding the specificities of physical devices and networking environment.

The SmartSensor infrastructure is an example of the recent research projects aimed at addressing the aforementioned issues, which is based on current standardization efforts for enabling WoT. This infrastructure was developed to manage a specific type of physical devices, those organized to shape a Wireless Sensor Networks (WSN). WSNs are networks consisting of tens to thousands of tiny devices capable to perform data sensing, processing, and wireless transmissions. Sensors work collaboratively, extracting environmental data and transmitting it to one or more exit points of the network, to be analyzed and further processed. Such WSNs are useful for a wide range of application domains and their usage has grown enormously in the last decade. Therefore, in the SmartSensor infrastructure, sensor generated data are considered as a primordial resource to be shared in the Web. In addition, SmartSensor considers all levels of integration previously mentioned. SmartSensor provides: (i) integration of distinct WSNs, i.e., consisting of sensor nodes that adopt different technologies, hardware and/or software; (ii) integration of WSN sensing data and functionality with other Web applications; and (iii) integration of WSN functionalities within a programming model that abstract the specificities of the WSN environment.

1.2 Goals

This book focuses on describing SmartSensor and how to develop applications for IoT/WoT using such an infrastructure. An application of parking management is adopted to illustrate the use of the SmartSensor infrastructure as an enabler technology for smart city solutions. This application was chosen due to the increasing parking problems in big cities as well as in mass events such as the Olympics, for instance. Although SmartSensor can be considered as a middleware for IoT, in its current version, it only provides communication and integration services as well as a programming model to develop applications on top of the WSN infrastructure. In the direction of providing a more broad view to the reader, we describe the requirements that a full functional middleware for IoT should meet and also present an overview of existent proposals for such a middleware.

1.3 Overview of the Book

The remainder of the book is organized as follows. Chapter 2 presents some background on the enabling technologies for IoT/WoT and on Middleware for IoT in terms of requirements and services. Chapter 3 introduces the SmartSensor infrastructure. Chapter 4 describes the Sensor Integration Module, while Chap. 5 details the Sensor Programming and Execution module. Chapter 6 presents a proof of concept developed with the SmartSensor, describing an application in the domain of smart buildings running on the infrastructure: the parking lot management. Chapter 7 contains our concluding remarks and future work.

References

1. Atzori, L., Lera, A., & Morabito, G. (2010). The internet of things: A survey. *Computer Networks*, *54*(15), 2787–2805.
2. Bandyopadhyay, D., & Sen, J. (2011, May). Internet of things—applications and challenges in technology and standardization. *Wireless Personal Communications*, *58*(1), 49–69.
3. Delicato, F. C., Pires, P. F., Pirmez, L., Batista, T. (2010). Wireless sensor networks as a service, 2010. *17th IEEE International Conference and Workshops* (pp. 410–417).
4. European Research Projects on the Internet of Things (CERP-IoT). (2009). *Internet of things— strategic research roadmap.*
5. Fielding, R. (2000). *Architectural styles and the design of network-based software architectures.* PhD thesis, University of California, Irvine.
6. Kortuem, G., Kawsar, F., Fitton, F., Sundramoorthy, V. (Jan/Feb 2010). Smart objects as building blocks for the internet of things. *IEEE Internet Computing*, *14*(1), 44–51.
7. Guinard, D. e Trifa, V. (2009). Towards the web of things: Web mashups for embedded devices. In *Proceedings of Workshop on Mashups, Enterprise Mashups and Lightweight Composition on the Web, International World Wide Web Conferences*. Madrid, Spain, 2009.
8. NIC (National Intelligence Council). (2008). Disruptive Civil Technologies Six Technologies with Potential Impacts on US Interests Out to 2025 Conference Report CR 2008–07, 2008. Retrieved from http://www.dni.gov/nic/NIC_home.html.
9. Pautasso, C., Zimmermann, O., Leymann, F. (2008). RESTful web services vs. web services: Making the right architectural decision. In *Proceedings of the 17th International Conference on World Wide Web, 2008*. Retrieved from http://portal.acm.org/citation.cfm?id=1367606.
10. Richardson, L., Ruby, S. (2008). *RESTful Web Services* (chap. 4, pp. 79–105). Sebastopol, CA: O'Reilly Media. Inc.
11. Santucci, G. (2009). From the internet to data to internet of things. *Proceedings of the International Conference on Future Trends of the Internet*.
12. Bandyopadhyay, S., Sengupta, M., Maiti, S., & Dutta, S. (2011, August). Role of middleware for internet of things: A study. *International Journal of Computer Science and Engineering Survey (IJCSES)*, *2*(3), 94–105.
13. Paridel, K., Bainomugisha, E., Vanrompay, Y., Berbers, Y., De Meuter, W. (2010). Middleware for the internet of things, design goals and challenges. *Electronic Communications of the EASST Journal*, *28*, 1–6.

Chapter 2
Basic Concepts

Abstract The *Web of Things* (WoT) paradigm is based on the use of protocols and standards widely accepted and already in use in the traditional Web, such as the *Hypertext Transfer Protocol* (HTTP) and the *Uniform Resource Identifier* (URI), to support information sharing and device interoperation. These standards combined with other elements such as the *Representational State Transfer* (REST) architectural pattern and the *Resource-oriented architecture* (ROA) allow sensed data, provided by the sensing physical devices via a *Wireless Sensor Networks* (WSN), to be treated as any other resource on the Web. Such physical devices are identified by URIs and accessed via HTTP basic operations (HTTP verbs). This Chapter briefly presents the main key concepts that support the WoT paradigm, such as wireless sensor networks, REST and ROA. We also discuss about the requirements that a middleware for IoT/WoT should meet and we give an overview of existing proposals for such a middleware.

Keywords Web of Things (WoT) · Wireless sensor networks (WSN) · Hypertext transfer protocol (HTTP) · Uniform resource identifier (URI) · Representational state transfer (REST) architecture · Resource-oriented architecture (ROA) · Middleware for IoT

2.1 Realizing the WoT Paradigm

According to Guinard et al. [9], the Web of Things (WoT) goes a step further in relation to the Internet of Things (IoT) as it integrates smart things not only to the Internet (the network), but also to the Web (application layer), allowing the development of applications built upon a myriad of networked physical elements. Section 2.1.1 discusses about the network infrastructure typically used in WoT to interconnect devices and physical objects, the Wireless Sensor Networks (WSN). Section 2.1.2 presents the application level elements that supports the development of applications built upon various networked physicalobjects.

F. C. Delicato et al., *Middleware Solutions for the Internet of Things*,
SpringerBriefs in Computer Science, DOI: 10.1007/978-1-4471-5481-5_2,
© The Author(s) 2013

2.1.1 *Wireless Sensor Networks*

To realize the idea of the WoT paradigm it is necessary to make the objects (things) addressable, searchable, controllable, and accessible via Web. Wireless Sensor Networks (WSNs), composed of sensors, actuators and embedded communication hardware, play a fundamental role in the connection of the physical and digital worlds as they monitor the physical devices, gathers their data and eventually act upon the environment. Sensors are typically capable of recognizing an event of interest and actuators can take an action accordingly. A WSN consists in a large number of nodes where data are collected by distributed and smart sensors associated to the devices. The sensing data is gathered to a *sink node* that sends the data to other computational devices, often more powerful, able to further processing the sensor produced data. As individual sensor nodes do not always have an Internet Protocol (IP) address, they cannot be directly accessible via Web. In this case, an intermediary element is used: the *Smart Gateways*. A Smart Gateway acts as a proxy between the objects and the Web, by communicating with the objects (in this case, the sensor nodes) and making them accessible via Web. Besides providing WSN nodes with accessibility through the Web, *Smart Gateways* also perform other functions such as to translate from Internet protocols to WSN communication protocols (and vice versa), and to provide added value information on top of the produced raw sensor data. Figure 2.1 illustrates the main elements of a WSN.

Nowadays, there are several hardware and software platforms for WSN available. In the SmartSensor infrastructure three different platforms are currently supported:

Fig. 2.1 Elements of a wireless sensor network connected to the WoT

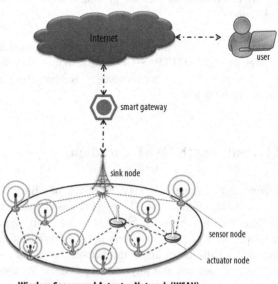

Wireless Sensor and Actuator Network (WSAN)

Arduino,[1] Sun SPOT,[2] and the MICA motes Family (manufactured by MEM-SIC,former Crossbow),[3] this later based on the TinyOS operating system,[4] specially designed to sensors. They are proper to a WSN scenario with several tiny and low-power networked devices in interaction.

Arduino refers to both a simple microprocessor board designed mainly for use by academics, and the software system that is used to program the board. The Arduino project was initiated in Ivrea Italy in 2005 to provide simple, easy-to-use boards, and it has been recently reported than more than 100,000 Arduino boards have been produced so far. The circuit design for the board is "open-source" in the sense that it is available under a Creative Commons license Attribution-ShareAlike 2.5 [4]. The board consists of an Atmel AVR processor—the latest boards contain the AVR Mega328 (8-bit processor, 32 Kbytes Flash, 2 KB SRAM, Digital I/O, PWM outputs, ADC inputs, SPI and UART communications, 16 MHz clock). Atmel AVR processors are used in many other motes due to their compact size, useful peripherals, and low-power sleep modes. A large range of peripherals is already available for Arduino, such as accelerometers, light, temperature sensors, motor drivers, and GPS receivers. The Arduino interface connectors provide direct connections to microprocessor pins such as digital I/O, analog I/O, interrupts and TTL-level UARTS. Different sensor interfaces can be quickly developed using the range of connectors. Arduino software is often developed using a simplified programming interface based on the Wiring project [3], and using a simple Integrated Development Environment (IDE). The system accepts code snippets that are automatically expanded into complete C/C++ programs, and compiled using a standard GNU tool-chain. A simple boot-loader automatically uploads code to the processor.

Sun SPOT (Small Programmable Object Technology) [22] is a platform developed by Sun Microsystems/Oracle. The Sun SPOT hardware platform is a small, battery operated wireless device, that runs the Squawk Java Virtual Machine directly on the processor without an underlying operating system. Sun SPOT provides a low-cost platform for the development of several wireless sensor and embedded applications. For instance, SPOTs can be used in robotics cars or in the monitoring of physical phenomena. There are two types of devices provided by SunSPOT: the free-range SPOTs (with processor, radio, sensor board and battery) and the base station (with processor and radio).

MEMSIC provides a broad portfolio of wireless sensor nodes to meet the specific needs of target applications for either end-user or OEM designs. It provides a variety of processor boards, sensor boards and data acquisition cards that connect to their wireless modules. Moreover, MEMSIC provides a wide range of gateway boards to connect to sensor nodes via multiple types of interfaces, including Ethernet, Wifi, USB and serial. All MICA and IRIS family sensor boards from MEMSIC support

---

[1] http://www.arduino.cc/

[2] http://www.sunspotworld.com/

[3] http://www.memsic.com/wireless-sensor-networks/

[4] http://www.tinyos.net/

TinyOS operating system. TinyOS is tiny and flexible operation system. It is the most used software platform for sensor networks, with approximately 25,000 downloads per year [14]. TinyOS uses a C dialect called nesC and defines a programing model based on independent and reusable components. It supports concurrency and flexible composition. Its main goals are minimizing resource use, by using as few hardware resources as possible, and preventing bugs. TinyOS provides a set of services for sensing, communication, storage, and temporization. Components can invoke and receive service requests, signal and receive events (such as, service finalization or hardware events), and schedule tasks. nesC implements the TinyOS component model. A nesC file allows the optimisation in code compilation to different sensor platforms.

2.1.2 HTTP, URI, REST, ROA

The integration of objects in the Web involves application protocols and architecture styles. At the application level, the HTTP protocol interoperability allows the seamless integration of objects with the Web. The REST architectural style, proposed by Fielding [8], enables that objects are modeled as *resources*, identified by URIs and accessed via HTTP. REST is built upon five principles:

1. Global identification of resources;
2. Uniform interface for acessing resources;
3. Self-descritive messages;
4. *Hypermedia as Engine of Application State*;
5. Stateless interactions.

The first principle refers to the identification of resources in requests by using URIs that provide a global address for resource and service discovery. A resource can be a server, a document, a Web page, a video stream, or a physical thing.

The second principle defines that the resources are avaliable via a uniform interface with a well-defined semantics [9]. The Hypertext Transfer Protocol (HTTP) offers a set of methods proper to enable the uniform interaction.

The self-descritive messages principle define the format of the messages exchanged between clients and servers. A resource can have several representations such as XML, JSON, HTML, etc. The specification of the representations that a cliente can receive is in the Accept field of the HTTP header, for instance, text/html (for HTML), application/xml (for XML) and application/json (for JSON).

The *Hypermedia as Engine Of Application State* (HATEOAS) is one of the core tenets of REST. It states that clients can control a Web application following hyperlinks. *Links* point to Web resources using the global identification (URIs). Clients follow links to explore a resource. In this schema, an application can be viewed as a state machine with pages representing a state and links representing the possible transitions.

The last REST principle defines that servers are *stateless*. This means that each request from clients contains all information (state) that the server needs to process it, including headers, URL, query parameters, etc. The ST part from the REST name means *State Transfer* that is embedded in the request's content. No information from the previous request is stored by the server. This principle is related to the scalability of the system as if a server maintain information for each user, its performance is affected in case of concurrent access [18].

The REST emphasis on resources is described by the *Resource–Oriented Architecture* (ROA) [19]. This means that resources are addressed using the standard description in the format of URIs, for instance: http://www.smartsensor.com/sensor1. URIs provide an unique identification to a resource, regardless of its type and representation. Thus, resources can be represented by means of various formats, such as Hyper-Text Markup Language (HTML), eXtended Markup Language (XML), JavaScript Object Notation (JSON), that are machine-readable and processable. REST offers a subset of HTTP commands to access and manipulate resources: GET, PUT, POST, DELETE. GET is used to retrieve information from a resource; POST is used to add new information; PUT is used to update information, writing to a resource; and DELETE is used to remove information. Thus, those standard Web operations enable the communication between the resources and the Web. REST requires that all resources (different physical devices) support this set of stateless methods to be accessable via Web. In this way, objects are abstracted as Web services [24]. Things conforming to the REST principles are called *RESTful*.

According to Zeng et al. [24], the use of the REST architecture in WoT is due to its low complexity and its loosing-coupling stateless interactions. In fact, several objects are resource-constrained devices and only a lightweight solution can be used for integrating them to the Web [9]. Once the resources are available in the Web, developers can create *mashups*, which are new Web applications composed by various elements, including virtual Web services and physical Web services provided by objects [9, 24]. As any Web 2.0 application, mashups are built based on a set of technologies (Atom [1], for instance), that supports the development of simple and highly interactive user interfaces. Mashups created by composing data and services of physical devices with other Web resources are called *physical mashups*. They focus on the reuse of real world objects with different applications [6, 9].

2.2 Middleware for IoT

The abovementioned technologies enable the connectivity of the objects to the Internet and make them accessible and manageable. However, to create value-added applications, by combining the resources connected to the Internet, a high abstraction level model needs to be used. Middleware platforms have been proposed [7, 11, 16, 17, 21] with the goal of facilitating the development of applications supporting the interoperability of interconnected devices, alleviating the programmer of the burden of dealing with the specificities of physical devices and networking environment. Through the use of middleware platforms, services may be provided on top of the resources connected to the Web, to facilitate the fast combination of features in order to create multiple value-added applications, the so-called *physical mashups* [5, 10].

The main requirements for a IoT middleware to enable the development of different applications domains include:

- fully interoperability support across heterogeneous devices in order to allow the things (smart objects) communicate with users, Internet services and among each other [15]. This is a challenge for realizing IoT due to the huge number of devices integrated in an IoT platform and their diversity in terms of data formats, protocols, nature of components, etc.
- the provision of a high-level Application Programming Interface(API) to transparently access the heterogeneous objects, hiding the specificities of the integrated devices. Such API may facilitate the creation of physical mashups.

According to Bandyopadhyay et al. [2], interoperation, device discovery and management, context detection, among others, are the main functional components of an IoT middleware. In addition, an application abstraction component is essential to support the communication with local and remote applications. Security and privacity, as well as the management of a massive data volume are other important functions of an IoT middleware.

In summary, an IoT middleware is a software artifact between the application layer and the infrastructure support (communication, processing, and sensing) offering a standardized means to acess data and services provided by the smart objects via a high level interface. Such a middleware also promotes the reuse of generic services that can be composed and configured to make easier the development of applications in a highly distributed and heterogeneous environment. Some works [2, 16] state that the middleware act as a glue between the applications and the heterogeneous devices.

In the following subsections we briefly presents some IoT middleware proposals.

2.2.1 UBIWARE

UBIWARE [16] is a agent-based middleware that represents each resource as a software agent. An agent is in charge of monitoring the condition of the resource, and enabling the interoperation of the resource with other elements. The main principles of UBIWARE is to allow automatic discovery, orchestration, choreography, invocation and execution of different Business Intelligence services. Communication, resource discovery and resource usage are performed via the correspondent agent.

The UBIWARE agent architecture consists of three layers [13]: (i) the Behavior Engine implemented in Java, (ii) a declarative middle-layer (Behavior Models corresponding to different roles the agent plays), and (iii) sensors and actuators, which are Java components.

Behavior models are represented in a high-level rule-based language, the *Semantic Agent Programming Language (SAPL)* [12], which is proposed by the UBIWARE team and it is based on the Resource Description Framework (RDF) [23] data model. The behavior engine parses an SPL document and loads it in the beliefs storage. Each agent has a behavior model. Interoperability between heterogeneous resources is achieved by semantic adaptation and by assigning a proactive agent to each of the resources.

Thus, this middleware is a multi-agent system where interoperability among the resources is supported by using agents, metadata and ontologies.

2.2.2 Hydra

The Hydra middleware [11] consists of a service-oriented architecture that relies on Web services to support the resource discovery, description and access based on XML and web protocols. It distinguishes resource restricted devices that are not able to host the middleware, and more powerful devices (Hydra-enabled devices). Each Hydra-enabled device hosts a Network Manager component, that is responsible for communication among devices. A proxy is used to connect the restricted devices to the Hydra network. Proxies are deployed on Hydra-enabled devices that act as gateways. Such proxies provide Web service interfaces for accessing a device.

The two main tasks performed by Hydra developers are: (i) integrating non-Hydra devices; and (ii) connecting Hydra-enabled devices to a network.

2.2.3 LinkSmart Middleware

The LinkSmart middleware [7], developed in the Hydra project, enables the integration of heterogeneous physical devices into applications via a Web service interface for controlling any type of physical device irrespective of its network technology such as Bluetooth, RF, ZigBee, RFID, WiFi, etc. The middleware name is different from the project name because it has been registered in Germany and used by the Hydra middleware, discussed in the previous subsection.

LinkSmart is based on a semantic model-driven architecture and enables the use of devices as services both by embedding services in devices and by proxy services for devices. The semantic description of devices is based on ontologies using OWL, OWL-s and SAWSDL.

2.2.4 OpenIoT

The OpenIoT project [21] provides an open-source middleware platform to enable the development of IoT applications according to a utility cloud computing delivery model. OPENIoT goal is to realize the idea of on demand access to IoT services offered over clouds of internet-connected objects, the so-called sensing as a service, providing a "cloud-of-things".

OpenIoT adheres to the W3C Semantic Sensor Networks (SSN) for describing sensors and also relies on the IETF Constrained Application Protocol (CoAP) [20] for the interaction with nodes and devices. The SSN ontology (Sensor and Sensor Network ontology) enables the specification of formal descriptions of sensor networks, thus allowing the semantic interoperability among networks.

As OpenIoT follows the REST principles, resources are addressed by URIs and can have different representation formats. HTTP operations are used to interact with the resources, through RESTful Web services.

2.2.5 Discussion

Despite the rising popularity of IoT and the emergence of several proposals of middleware for IoT, the state-of-the-art of such proposals shows that they are still under development. They share the ideia of seamlessly integrating a broad range of heterogeneous devices and offering a high level mechanism to enable developers to build IoT applications without having to deal with heterogeneity issues.

A brief comparison of the abovementioned proposals shows that: (i) most proposals rely on ontologies to address the semantic interoperability between the sensed data; (ii) the use of well-established Web services technologies is adopted by some IoT middleware such as Hydra and OpenIoT. Both works highlight the importance of following popular and emerging standards for IoT.

In summary, several issues remain opened, as discussed in [2], such as a fully support for context detection and processing and for managing high volumes of sensed data. According to Bandyopadhyay et al. [2], the current challenge is to provide a generic IoT middleware, applicable across multiple domains.

References

1. Atom Enable. (2004). Disponvel em http://www.atomenabled.org/
2. Bandyopadhyay, S., Sengupta, M., Maiti, S., & Dutta, S. (August 2011). Role of middleware for internet of things: A study. *International Journal of Computer Science and Engineering Survey (IJCSES), 2*(3), 94–105
3. Barragn, H. Wiring project http://wiring.org.co/
4. Creative Commons. Creative commons license attribution-sharealike 2.5 generic version. http://creativecommons.org/licenses/by-sa/2.5/
5. Delicato, F. C., Pires, P. F., Pirmez, L., & Batista, T. (2010). Wireless sensor networks as a service. In *17th IEEE International Conference and Workshops*, (pp. 410–417).
6. Duquennoy, S., Grimaud, G., & Vandewalle, J. (2009). The web of things: Interconnecting devices with high usability and performance. In *International Conferences on Embedded Software and Systems*. Retrieved April 2013, from http://ieeexplore.ieee.org/stamp/stamp.jsp?tp=&arnumber=5066664

7. Eisenhauer, M., Rosengren, P., & Antolin, P. (2009). A development platform for integrating wireless devices and sensors into ambient intelligence systems.
8. Fielding, R. (2000). Architectural styles and the design of network-based software architectures (PhD thesis, University of California, Irvine).
9. Guinard, D., Trifa, V., & Wilde, E. (2010). *Architecting a mashable open world wide web of things*. Technical Report, 663. Institute for Pervasive Computing. Retrieved April 2013, from http://www.bibsonomy.org/bibtex/2dcc3fabe2de456144254afdcc8e06776/flint63
10. Guinard, D., Trifa, V., Pham, T., & Liechti, O. (June 2009). Towards physical mashups in the web of things. In *Proceedings of IEEE Sixth International Conference on Networked Sensing Systems*. Pittsburgh, USA.
11. Jahn, M., Pramudianto, F., & Akkad, A. (September 2009). Hydra middleware for developing pervasive systems: A case study in the e-Health domain. In *1st International Workshop on Distributed Computing in Ambient Environments (DiComAe 2009)* (pp. 15–18). Paderborn, Germany.
12. Katasonov, A., & Terziyan, V. (2007). SmartResource platform and semantic agent programming language (S-APL). In P. Petta et al. (Eds.), *Proceedings of the 5-th German Conference on Multi-Agent System Technologies (MATES'07), 24–26 September, 2007, LNAI 4687* (pp. 25–36). Leipzig: Springer.
13. Khriyenko, O., & Nagy, M. (2011). Semantic web-driven agent-based ecosystem for linked data and services. In *Service Computation 2011: The Third International Conferences on Advanced Service, Computing*.
14. Levis, P. Experiences from a decade of tinyOS development. http://www.tinyos.net
15. Mattern, F., & Floerkemeier, C. (2010). From the internet of computers to the internet of things. In K. Sachs, I. Petrov, & P. Guerrero (Eds.), *From active data management to event-based systems and more* (pp. 242–259). Heidelberg: Springer.
16. Nagy, M., Katasonov, A., Khriyenko, O., Nikitin, S., Szydlowski, M., & Terzivan, V. Challenges of middleware for the internet of things. In A. D. Rodi (Ed.), *Automation Control—Theory and Practice*, ISBN: 978-953-307-039-1, InTech, doi:10.5772/7869. Available from: http://www.intechopen.com/books/automation-control-theory-and-practice/challenges-of-middleware-for-the-internet-of-things
17. Paridel, K., Bainomugisha, E., Vanrompay, Y., Berbers, Y., & De Meuter, W. (2010). Middleware for the internet of things, design goals and challenges. *Electronic Communications of the EASST Journal, 28*.
18. Pautasso, C., Zimmermann, O., & Leymann, F. (2008). RESTful web Services versus big web services: Making the right architectural decision. In *Proceedings of the 17th international conference on World Wide Web*. Disponvel em http://portal.acm.org/citation.cfm?id=1367606. Acessado em 02 de Dezembro de 2010.
19. Richardson L., & Ruby, S. (2008). *RESTful web services* (pp. 79–105). OReilly Media, cap. 4.
20. Shelby, Z., Frank, B., & Sturek, D. (May 2011). Constrained application protocol (CoAP). http://datatracker.ietf.org/doc/draft-ietf-core-coap/
21. Soldatos, J., Serrano, M., & Hauswirth, M. (2012). Convergence of utility computing with the internet-of-things. In *proceedings of the2012 Sixth International Conference on Innovative Mobile and Internet Services in Ubiquitous, Computing (IMIS'12)* (pp. 874–879).
22. Sun SPOT World. (2011). Retrieved April 2013, from http://www.sunspotworld.com/
23. W3C. (2008). SPARQL protocol and RDF query language. http://www.w3.org/TR/rdf-sparql-query/
24. Zeng, D., Guo, S., & Cheng, Z. (Sep 2011). The web of things: A survey. *Journal of Communications, 6*(6), 424–438. doi:10.4304/jcm.6.6.424-438.

Chapter 3
SmartSensor: An Infrastructure for the Web of Things

Abstract In order to fast populate the Web of Things, approaches based on ubiquitous protocols and standards are attractive to promote interoperability among heterogeneous devices and to facilitate the development of applications on top of such devices. In this context, this Chapter presents SmartSensor, an infrastructure for WoT built at the middleware layer and based on current efforts of standardization, with the main purpose of integrating Wireless Sensor Networks (WSNs) to the Web in a transparent, seamless and flexible way. By integrating WSNs to the Web via SmartSensor, sensor-generated data can be provided to client applications or users exactly in the same way as documents or other Web resources. Furthermore, SmartSensor considers the emerging scenario where multiple WSNs from different technologies and owners are integrated in a unique, virtual sensing infrastructure, enabling data from different networks to be provided to various applications running on top of them. In this Chapter, the infrastructure architecture and operation are briefly presented, emphasizing the features that make SmartSensor fully complaint to the WoT paradigm.

Keywords Internet of Things (IoT) · Web of Things (WoT) · Wireless sensor networks · REST · HTTP · SmartSensor architecture

3.1 Overview

Current approaches to integrate smart devices to the Internet have several drawbacks, and alternative architectures need to be proposed and evaluated so that the Web of Things (WoT) paradigm is fully realized. In particular, in order to fast populate the Web of Things, approaches based on ubiquitous protocols and standards would promote interoperability among heterogeneous devices acting as data providers, and facilitate the development of applications that make use of such data. In this context, this Chapter presents SmartSensor, an infrastructure for the WoT built at the

F. C. Delicato et al., *Middleware Solutions for the Internet of Things*,
SpringerBriefs in Computer Science, DOI: 10.1007/978-1-4471-5481-5_3,
© The Author(s) 2013

middleware layer and based on current efforts of standardization, with the main purpose of integrating Wireless Sensor Networks (WSNs) [1] to the Web. SmartSensor is a project developed under the sponsorship of the Brazilian National Network for Education and Research (RNP – *Rede Nacional de Ensino e Pesquisa*[1]).

In the SmartSensor project, unlike other existing initiatives [8, 9, 11, 14, 22] that deal with the addressability and availability of all types of smart objects, the main focus is in integrating Wireless Sensor Networks in the Web. Furthermore, SmartSensor considers the emerging scenario where multiple WSNs from different technologies and owners are integrated in a unique, virtual sensing infrastructure, enabling data from different networks to be provided to various applications running on top of them. In such scenario, the WSN itself is seen as a service (WSN as a Service [3]), and it is possible to take full advantage of the physical infrastructure of sensor nodes already deployed, sharing the communication and sensing resources, thus potentially increasing the return of investment (ROI) for the infrastructure owners and generating added value for the end users [16, 35].

The adoption of the SmartSensor infrastructure allows WSNs to be integrated to the Web in a transparent, seamless and flexible way. By integrating WSNs to the Web via SmartSensor, sensor-generated data can be provided to client applications or users exactly in the same way as documents or other Web resources. Following the Web architecture, a resource should have a uniform resource identifier (URI) [28] and by using URIs it is possible to navigate to/from resources and also to link resources. It is possible to have different representations for the same resource, which is a very powerful concept, i.e. a server can provide HTML content for human consumption and eXtensible Markup Language (XML) [36] or Java Script Object Notation (JSON) for machines. In WSNs, a resource can represent either an individual sensor reading, the aggregate information from a set of sensors, from the whole WSN or even from different networks connected to the infrastructure. Moreover, sensor data can be composed with information originated from other devices and/or applications that are available in the Web, in order to deliver value-added information to the end user. Basically, resources are consumed in the Web by two types of clients: (i) end users, that interact through a Web page displayed by a browser, or (ii) client applications. Such applications can be SOAP or REST-based Web services, or mashup applications, in either case implementing an application-to-application interaction.

SmartSensor was designed from scratch to be complaint with the WoT paradigm, thus it was built on REST (Representational State Transfer) [6] principles and relies on current Web standards and protocols, such as HTTP (Hypertext Transfer Protocol) [25, 26] and URIs (Uniform Resource Identifier). In WoT, the HTTP protocol is not only used as a communication protocol to carry data formatted according to any specification (as in the case of Web services technologies). Instead, HTTP is used as the standard mechanism to support all interactions with smart objects. This interaction occurs through the HTTP main operations (GET, POST, PUT and DELETE i.e. the verbs of REST), that provide a well-defined interface to expose the functionality of the objects in the Web. Such interface complies with the REST principles [6, 8],

---

[1] http://www.rnp.br/en/

thus allowing that the services of smart objects are accessed as resources in an ROA (Resource-Oriented Architecture) approach [12, 17]. Besides the standardization and simplification in the process of applications development, the use of the HTTP protocol also eliminates compatibility issues between different manufacturers, proprietary protocols and data formats [4]. Such feature is particularly appealing in the integration of WSN to the Web, since the devices that compose such networks are heterogeneous regarding their software and hardware technologies.

To make a WSN Web-enabled is not a trivial task as a consequence of the differences between Internet applications and WSN applications. WSN applications have specific Quality of Services (QoS) requirements and data delivery models. They run on battery operated devices which most of the time sleep and wakeup only when there is data to be exchanged. Furthermore, the WSN protocol stack is very different from the Internet stack and the multicast and asynchronous communication is the most frequent style in comparison to the unicast and synchronous approach of standard Internet applications [34]. Therefore, there are several issues to be addressed by a middleware-layer infrastructure to provide WSN as a service in the WoT.

The Web of Things paradigm exposes the functionalities of smart devices in the Web using two different approaches and both were adopted in the SmartSensor infrastructure. In the first approach, embedded Web servers are deployed directly within smart objects, enabling that the features of these devices are available in the Web as RESTful resources [21, 29]. However, whenever a smart object does not have enough hardware resources to run an embedded server, a different approach for the WoT integration is required, based on the adoption of a WoT Gateway or Smart Gateway. Gateways are (more) powerful devices used as a bridge to provide the functionalities of smart devices through a RESTful interface. Gateways have two basic functions: to provide a RESTful interface with URIs that identify and provide access to physical objects (smart devices) and their resources; and to realize the communication with physical objects by using their specific APIs. Gateways intercept HTTP request messages issued by client applications and perform any conversion of data and protocols before forwarding the converted messages to the WSN devices. In the same way, messages sent by the sensor nodes in response to application requests are translated by the gateways to the HTTP format. A gateway can support multiple types of devices through an architecture encompassing a set of drivers responsible for solving heterogeneity issues.

Smart Gateways can also be used to perform more complex operations with data obtained from a WSN, and to orchestrate the composition of a highest level Web application from several lower-level services provided by devices. These Web applications are the so-called *physical mashups* created from the composition of information provided by devices available as resources through the RESTful API provided by the gateway [10]. As a basic example of this type of application lets consider a set of devices connected to the Web that provide power consumption monitoring of electronic appliances. The Smart Gateway could provide a service that presents a map showing the geographical location of several sensor instrumented buildings (Smart Buildings [7, 13, 30]) and then, whenever a user selects a particular building, the service returns the consolidate energy consumption monitored by all devices in such building. The construction and deployment of physical mashups is a feature of WoT with the appealing potential to provide value-added services to the end user, and influence the creation of new business models and applications.

3.2 The SmartSensor Architecture

The SmartSensor architecture encompasses three main software modules (Fig. 3.1): (i) *Sensor Integration Module* (SIM), responsible for the integration of sensor devices from different software and hardware technologies, (ii) *Programming and Execution Module* (PEM), responsible for providing additional functionality on top of SIM, in particular the ability to compose value-added services from the information provided by Web-enabled devices and to search for available services, and (iii) *Web 3.0 Integration Module* (WIM), responsible for integrating devices with Web 3.0 applications and platforms [31]. In this Book we will first briefly describe these three components and then we will further detail SIM and PEM.

Fig. 3.1 SmartSensor modules

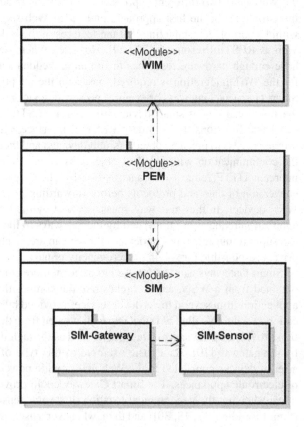

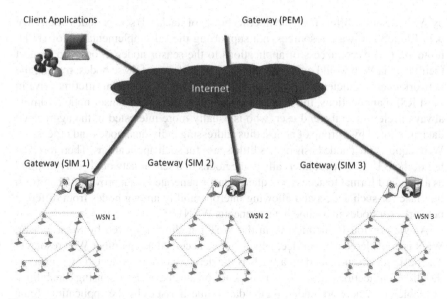

Fig. 3.2 SmartSensor environment

The SmartSensor is a system composed of a group of potentially heterogeneous wireless sensor networks, a set of gateway nodes organized in a hierarchy, and several client applications (Fig. 3.2). Each WSN is connected to the infrastructure through one gateway node. Gateway nodes communicate among them so that the Smart-Sensor keeps a unified view on the resources provided by all WSNs connected to the infrastructure. Such unified view is managed by the Programming and Execution Module (PEM) while the Sensor Integration Module (SIM) is responsible for managing the resources of a single WSN.

The software components of the *Sensor Integration Module* are deployed and executed in both the sensor nodes and the gateway nodes. PEM and WIM components execute only in the gateway nodes. Considering the traditional architecture of a WSN, the gateway corresponds to the Sink node. Besides the software components of SIM, PEM and WIM, a gateway node needs to implement the WSN radio protocol stack (MAC and physical layers) in order to enable the communication with the sensor nodes, thus acting as a bridge between the Internet protocols and WSN protocols. Most of the current sensor platforms adopt IEEE 802.15.4 protocol (ZigBee [27]) to communicate.

The Sensor Integration Module includes, among other software components, those responsible for the implementation of the HTTP protocol API, as well as drivers for handling received requests and specific commands of each sensor platform connected to the infrastructure. The gateway is responsible for integrating WSNs in the Web, extracting data from them, and providing such data to end users or client applications. The use of a gateway node is ultimately required in spite of sensor nodes having or not an embedded HTTP server, for the following reasons: (i) the protocol stack adopted by WSNs usually differs from the Internet protocol stack; (ii) sensor nodes often have very limited hardware resources, not supporting the full implementation of HTTP protocol; (iii) direct access of applications to the sensor nodes in order to request their data via Web would quickly drain energy resources of those nodes, making the network energy efficiency quite poor and decreasing its operating lifetime; (iv) in most RSSF applications, the data provided by one individual sensor node is almost always irrelevant to the end user, who is usually more interested in the aggregated data monitored by a group of nodes; thus addressing individual nodes and processing Web requests on a node basis makes little sense for such applications. Therefore, the use of the HTTP protocol internally to the nodes of a sensor network is only justified as a standard format to access and query sensor generated data, providing a uniform interface for such access and allowing interoperability among nodes from different networks (or nodes in a same heterogeneous WSN).

As we previously mentioned, in the WoT paradigm followed by SmartSensor, WSN is considered as a service, which can be accessed as any other Web resource. The basic service provided by a WSN is the delivery of data collected by sensors to the client applications. Such delivery depends on the discovery of sensing capabilities available in the network nodes, on the data requests issues by the applications (data consumers) and on the strategy of the provider nodes to communicate their data to the application. Considering this general scenario of a WSN operation, the functionalities of SIM are executed in a series of phases that are intertwined with the WSN working itself. These phases are: (i) service discovery; (ii) submission of application requests; and (iii) data collection and delivery. The identification of the WSN operation phases guided the specification of SIM logical architecture as well as the implementation of its components both in the gateway side and in the sensor nodes side. In the WoT paradigm, an abstraction of the WSN data delivery service is provided to the application, so that the network can be accessed and eventually configured according to each application needs, like any other resource available in the Web. For this purpose, a uniform interface to access the WSN is provided, adopting the REST architectural principles implemented via HTTP protocol.

Regarding the Programming and Execution Module (PEM), its main purpose is to allow end users to quickly compose value-added services, and to efficiently search for services provided by Web-enabled WSNs. PEM encompasses *Publishing and Discovery*, *Data Manager*, and *EMML Scripts Manager* components (Fig. 3.3). The services offered by a WSN are published and discovered through a gateway, and described by using XML.

PEM offers a Domain Specific Language (DSL) for programming Web mashup applications specifically tailored for the WSN environment. The adopted DSL is an extension of the Enterprise Mashup Markup language (EMML) [5]. EMML is a declarative language for developing Web mashups that provides portability and interoperability of developed programs, also allowing the integration of data from different sources. EMML is an open language based on XML, made available in the public domain by the Open Mashup Alliance (OMA) [18]. Applications created by using EMML produce new data that can be used in other applications and other mashups, thus allowing a high degree of reusability. This language allows the

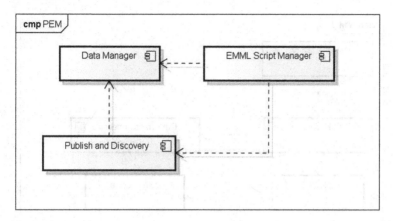

Fig. 3.3 PEM components

composition of mashups with traditional Web services (based on SOAP, third party APIs or REST, for instance) and SQL databases. OMA provides the EMML specification, the EMML schema; and an open source implementation of reference, which allows processing EMML scripts. An EMML file is a mashup script written in EMML.

Finally, the Web 3.0 Integration Module (WIM) integrates smart objects with Web 3.0 applications and platforms, so as to promote interactivity and data sharing; specially allowing the building of physical Web mashups encompassing information provided by real world devices and enriched with semantic information. WIM allows the publication of data provided by WSNs following Linked Open Data (LOD) principles [15]. LOD [14] is a set of best practices for publishing and connecting structured data sets on the Web, in order to create a "Web of Data". Published data that follow the LOD principles have well-defined structure and semantics, allowing its processing by computational methods. According to the principles [15], data published in the Web must be in RDF (Resource Description Framework [24]) format. RDF is a family of W3C (World Wide Web Consortium) specifications, used as a general method for conceptual description or data modelling. LOD can help dealing with the growing volume of sensed data, thus contributing to the deployment of large-scale WSNs. On the other hand, by interconnecting sensor data with other types of data, such as environmental and sociological data, enhanced information can be delivered to the end user or application. Some proposals for publishing sensor data by following the LOD principles can be seen in [2, 14, 19, 20]. These proposals do not consider, in general, intrinsic characteristics of WSN such as limited energy, asynchronous communication and low processing capacity. Thus, the WIM module of the SmartSensor infrastructure extends and adapts the LOD principles for integration of sensor data. The five main components of this module are (Fig. 3.4): (i) *Data Capture*, responsible for receiving data and metadata sent from one or more WSNs; (ii) *Data Transformation*, responsible for transforming the sensor data received from

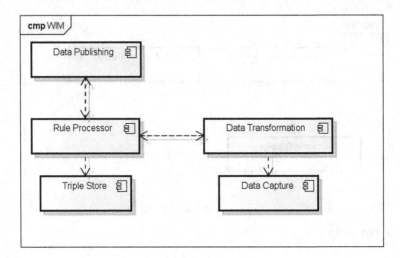

Fig. 3.4 WIM components

a WSN to the RDF format; (iii) *Rule Processor*, responsible for the construction and execution of logical rules that initiate predefined actions which, when activated, coordinate the delivery and storage of data and enable data fusion using simple arithmetic operators; (iv) *Triple-Store (or triples repository)* responsible for storing (for later use) sensor data converted to RDF; and (v) *Asynchronous Data Publisher*, which is responsible for sending sensed data, already converted to the RDF format, for users that have registered interest in receiving them, thus creating an asynchronous stream of sensor data in RDF.

WIM acts as a hub in the Web, obtaining data and metadata from WSNs integrated to SmartSensor and publishing these data based on LOD principles. The publishing of sensor data can be done in two different ways. The first one is by issuing queries formatted in SPARQL [32]or in RDF Query Language [23] in order to recovery data generated at the query time. SPARQL is a standard query language recommended by W3C to recover data from RDF graphs. The second way is through an asynchronous communication mechanism where a user provides a communication interface and a push rule. Whenever the parameters that satisfy the condition of a defined rule are met, data in RDF format is sent to the respective user along with a reference (via URIs) for the provenance information (indicating which network has produced the delivery data).

3.3 Exposing WSN as REST Resources in the SmartSensor

As extensively seen throughout this Book, in the Web of Things paradigm all the functionalities provided by connected devices are accessed as RESTful resources via Universal Resource Identifiers (URIs). Thus, as already mentioned, the resources of a sensor node, a set of nodes, a WSN, or a set of WSNs associated with a gateway must be accessed via URI. A URI is used to locate a specific gateway, to identify a device on a network, and to specify a resource provided by a device [17]. Each node in a WSN is endowed with a number of sensing units (light, temperature, accelerometer, etc.), a number of actuators (digital outputs, leds, etc.) and a number of internal components (radio, battery). All these parts (including the nodes themselves) are the resources of the REST architecture. Resources are organized in a tree hierarchy and each of them implements or inherits the four verbs of the HTTP protocol. In the SmartSensor infrastructure, the URI to access a resource provided by a sensor node has the general format http://gateway IP address and port/ identification of the type of the driver/node ID/node resource. The gateway IP address uniquely identifies the specific gateway in the Web; the driver identification indicates the type of the WSN platform associated with the gateway that the client wants to access; the identification of the node indicates the specific device associated with the gateway that is to be accessed (such node ID can be created locally or be a portion of the MAC address of the sensor, depending on the WSN platform used); finally, the node resource specified in the URI indicates which functionality of the node the client wants to access. For example, the access to the temperature reading from a sensor node of Sun SPOT platform [33] whose last four digits of MAC address (used as node ID in such platform) are "1265" can be done through the URI http://localhost:8888/ spotserver/spot-1265/light where "/light" identifies the required type of the node resource.

This usage of URI also allows the system to provide links for clients to browse between sub resources of a resource. For example, a request sent to the following URL http://localhost:8888/spotserver/spot-1265 returns a list with links to all available resources in this node (SPOT). These links allow clients to access any specific resource and also to navigate from the representation of the state of a resource to other representations of different resources. Furthermore, it is also possible to use links to guide the client in the various interactions that can be performed with the resource.

Regarding to the representation of resources, WSN devices connected to the SmartSensor infrastructure can be represented in XML, HTML and JSON. The HTML representation was adopted to simplify human interaction with the available resources, enabling navigation within the structure of resources through links to sub resources (also called child resources). In response to a Web request via the provided URI, the gateway may return an HTML page containing a list of the connected devices separated by type. Each device in the list has as associated link that allows the user to access such device (and its provided services/resources). In most cases, however, a XML file is returned in response to the HTTP request, allowing an application-to-application interaction. Finally, JSON format is also available for representing the resources returned in response to an HTTP request. JSON (Java Script Object Notation) is a lightweight alternative to the XML as a data interchange format [10]. It is a text-based open standard for data client/server data exchange and it is used whenever it is necessary to decrease the footprint of the application, for instance, to exchange data among sensor nodes that have an embedded server. For instance, in the SmartSensor infrastructure the server implemented in Sun SPOT nodes responds to HTTP requests by sending the sensor readings embedded into a JSON file. An example of the payload in a reply message in JSON is the following: "sensor": "1265", "temp": "27.75", "scale": "celsius", "timestamp": "Wed Jun 22 16:12:13 BRT 2011" where the sensor is recognized by the last four digits of its MAC address, temp is the temperature resource with its current value.

3.4 Accessing and Using WoT-Enabled WSNs Through the SmartSensor

In the SmartSensor infrastructure there is a hierarchy of gateway nodes, each one containing a Web server. PEM components execute in a gateway node responsible for keeping and providing the unified view of all WSNs integrated to the WoT infrastructure, while SIM components run in a gateway node connected to a single WSN. The PEM Web server is kept always up-and-running waiting for requests in a well-known URL. Upon start-up, the SIM Gateway publishes its current IP address and port number to the PEM server. It also sends to the PEM the list of resources it has currently available (set of connected WSNs). Upon initialization, each sensor node in a WSN that wishes to connect to the SmartSensor should send an advertising message to the SIM Gateway. In the SmartSensor current implementation the multihop communication is not supported. Therefore, advertising messages are broadcasted in the network and it is assumed that every node is in the gateway radio communication range. Such messages are discarded by every other node except the gateway, which will process the content and update its database of resources. Periodically, the gateway exchanges messages with the PEM to inform the current available resources. Interactions with the resources provided by the SmartSensor infrastructure may occur basically in two ways. A client that is interested in building mashup applications on top of the WSN provided resources interacts only through PEM. For this type of user, the source of a given resource (the specific WSN the data comes from) remains transparent, since he/she is only interested in using resources that match to a description (geographic location, type of sensor, etc.). A client that is interested in directly accessing the resources provided by a WSN interacts through the SIM.

A given user discovers the resources of all available WSNs integrated to the SmartSensor infrastructure by accessing the PEM. To do this, the SmartSensor infrastructure provides a REST-based discovery service through the URI: http://PEM_server:8080/pem-v3.4-emml/listSIMEMML. This service returns an XML file (Fig. 3.5) containing all the WSNs currently registered in SmartSensor, indicating the IP address of the gateway for each network. Once the user gets the IP of a given desired network (Gateways IP), he/she can find out what resources are available in that specific network. For doing this, there is another REST Web service provided by SIM and accessed through: http://SIM_server/gateway/rest/GetServices/. This service returns all resources offered by the given network, informing the sensorsÍDs (optionally), and the types of sensing data they collect. With this information users

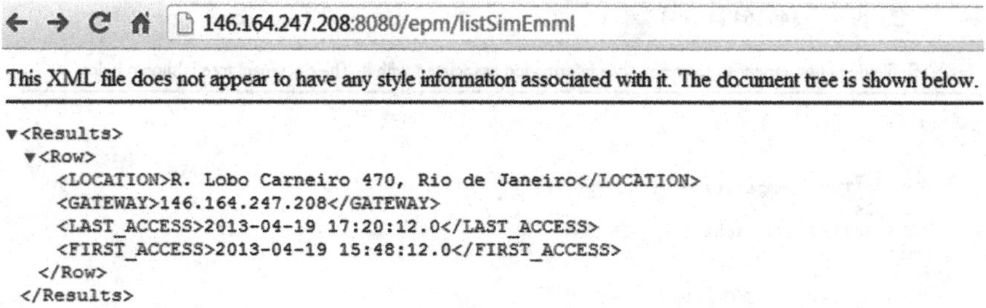

← → C ⌂ 🗋 146.164.247.208:8080/epm/listSimEmml

This XML file does not appear to have any style information associated with it. The document tree is shown below.

```
▼<Results>
  ▼<Row>
    <LOCATION>R. Lobo Carneiro 470, Rio de Janeiro</LOCATION>
    <GATEWAY>146.164.247.208</GATEWAY>
    <LAST_ACCESS>2013-04-19 17:20:12.0</LAST_ACCESS>
    <FIRST_ACCESS>2013-04-19 15:48:12.0</FIRST_ACCESS>
    </Row>
  </Results>
```

Fig. 3.5 REST service provided by PEM to discover the WSNs registered in the SmartSensor

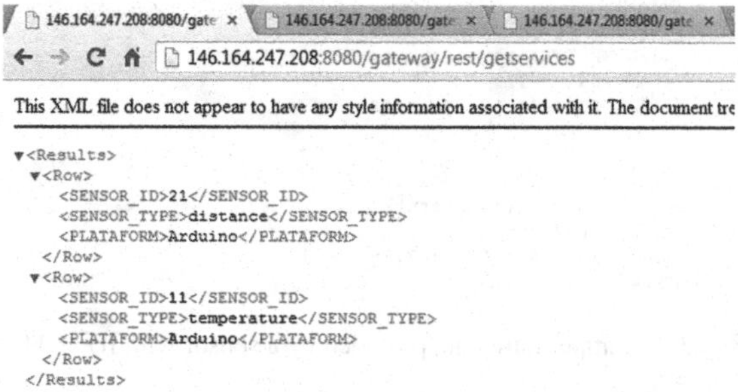

Fig. 3.6 XML file returned as the output of a call to GetServices representing the services provided by a WSN connected to the SmartSensor

🗋 146.164.247.208:8080/gate × 🗋 146.164.247.208:8080/gate × 🗋 146.164.247.208:8080/gate ×

← → C ⌂ 🗋 146.164.247.208:8080/gateway/rest/getservices

This XML file does not appear to have any style information associated with it. The document tre

```
▼<Results>
  ▼<Row>
    <SENSOR_ID>21</SENSOR_ID>
    <SENSOR_TYPE>distance</SENSOR_TYPE>
    <PLATAFORM>Arduino</PLATAFORM>
    </Row>
  ▼<Row>
    <SENSOR_ID>11</SENSOR_ID>
    <SENSOR_TYPE>temperature</SENSOR_TYPE>
    <PLATAFORM>Arduino</PLATAFORM>
    </Row>
  </Results>
```

can obtain the information (sensing data) already stored in the SIM database, or make a new request for data. Figure 3.6 shows an XML file representing an example of the outcome of a call to GetServices that presents the services (type of sensor data) offered by a given WSN connected to the SmartSensor. In this example the nodes (from Arduino platform) provides temperature and distance services.

To find out which sensors are available in a given WSN that provide data of a specific type, SmartSensor provides other service, accessed via URI: http://SIM_server/ gateway/rest/getdata/type_of_sensor. Then, the user can send a request to a specific node to perform a specific service, by using the generic URI: http://SIM_server/ gateway/rest/request/id_sensor/type_of_sensor; or he/she can request data from a specific type (for instance, light, temperature, acceleration, etc) from a given WSN without specifying any particular node (this is the most frequent case in WSNs). Figure 3.7 shows an XML file with historical temperature data returned from a request for the temperature service of a specific node (in this example, node with ID = 11).

Besides the types of sensing data available in the sensor nodes, other relevant metadata are kept in the SIM database (more details on this in Chap. 4), such as QoS parameters, geographical location, among others. However, in the current implementation of SmartSensor, only searches for types of sensors or for specific nodes are available.

The interactions within the domain of a given WSN occur basically as follows (Fig. 3.8). Suppose a request from a client application is sent to the SIM Gateway, which is continuously listening for incoming requests. This part of communication

← → C ⌂ □ **146.164.247.208**:8080/epm/request?sim=146.164.247.208&service=temperature&id=11

This XML file does not appear to have any style information associated with it. The document tree is shown below.

```
▼<Results>
  ▼<Row>
     <SENSOR_ID>11</SENSOR_ID>
     <SENSOR_TYPE>temperature</SENSOR_TYPE>
     <DATA>24</DATA>
     <DATE>2013-04-19 14:51:57</DATE>
   </Row>
  ▼<Row>
     <SENSOR_ID>11</SENSOR_ID>
     <SENSOR_TYPE>temperature</SENSOR_TYPE>
     <DATA>34</DATA>
     <DATE>2013-04-19 14:54:32</DATE>
   </Row>
  ▼<Row>
     <SENSOR_ID>11</SENSOR_ID>
     <SENSOR_TYPE>temperature</SENSOR_TYPE>
     <DATA>34</DATA>
     <DATE>2013-04-19 14:54:33</DATE>
   </Row>
  ▼<Row>
     <SENSOR_ID>11</SENSOR_ID>
     <SENSOR_TYPE>temperature</SENSOR_TYPE>
     <DATA>30</DATA>
     <DATE>2013-04-19 14:57:14</DATE>
   </Row>
```

Fig. 3.7 Temperature data provided by a sensor with ID = 11

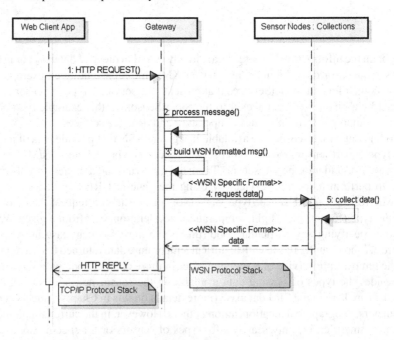

Fig. 3.8 Overview of the interactions in the SmartSensor

is performed using the traditional TCP/IP protocol stack between the application and the gateway. Once the gateway receives the HTTP request, the SIM components process the message content and then build a new message in the specific format of the WSN platform whose nodes need to be tasked to meet the request. This new message in the format understood by the sensor nodes is sent through a serial cable that connects the desktop computer to the wireless communication component (part of the gateway implementation that acts as the WSN sink node). The message is then forwarded over radio to the sensor nodes by broadcast and will be accepted by those nodes whose ID matches the one specified in the request or by all nodes if the broadcast address was specified in the request. Upon reception of the request, the sensors perform the necessary actions the request demands, generating the reply messages in the networks specific format. Reply messages sent by the sensors are processed in the gateway and translated to HTTP/TCP/IP format before sent back to the requiring application.

References

1. Akyildiz, I. F., et al. (October 2004). Wireless sensor and actor networks: research challenges. *Ad Hoc Networks Journal (Elsevier)*, 2(4), 351–367.
2. Brring, A., Janowicz, K., Stasch, C., Schade, S., & Llaves, A. (2011). Demonstration: A RESTful SOS Proxy for Linked Sensor Data. In *Semantic Sensor Networks 2011* (pp. 112–115).
3. Delicato, F. C., Pires, P. F., Pirmez, L., & Batista, T. (2010). Wireless sensor networks as a service, In *2010 17th IEEE International Conference and Workshops* (pp. 410–417).
4. Duquennoy, S., Grimaud, G., & Vandewalle, J. (2009). The web of things: interconnecting devices with high usability and performance. In *International Conferences on Embedded Software and Systems*, Last access April 2013, http://ieeexplore.ieee.org/stamp/stamp.jsp?tp=&arnumber=5066664.
5. EMML. (2010). Enterprise mashup markup language, Open Mashup Alliance. Last access April 2013, http://www.openmashup.org/.
6. Fielding, R. (2000). Architectural styles and the design of network-based software architectures (PhD thesis, University of California, Irvine).
7. Fortino, G., & Guerrieri, A. (2011). Decentralized and embedded management for smart buildings, In *Proceedings of the Workshop on Applications of Software Agents, WASA '11* (pp. 3–7).
8. Guinard, D., & Trifa, V. (2009). Towards the web of things: web mashups for embedded devices. In *Proceedings of Workshop on Mashups, Enterprise Mashups and Lightweight Composition on the Web*. Madrid, Spain: International World Wide Web Conferences.
9. Guinard, D. (2010). Towards opportunistic applications in a web of things. In *IEEE International Conference on Pervasive Computing and Communications Workshops*.
10. Guinard, D., Trifa, V., Pham, T., & Liechti, O. (June 2009). Towards physical mashups in the web of things. In *Proceedings of IEEE Sixth International Conference on Networked Sensing Systems*. Pittsburgh, USA.
11. Guinard, D., Trifa, V., & Wilde, E. (2010). *Architecting a Mashable Open World Wide Web of Things*. Technical Report, 663. Institute for Pervasive Computing. Last access April 2013, http://www.bibsonomy.org/bibtex/2dcc3fabe2de456144254afdcc8e06776/flint63.
12. Guo, X., Shen J., & Yin Z. (2010). On software development based on SOA and ROA. In *Control and Decision Conference (CCDC)* (pp. 1032–1035). Publishing Press.
13. Byun, J., & Park, S. (2011). Development of a self-adapting intelligent system for building energy saving and context-aware smart services. *IEEE Transactions on Consumer Electronics*, 57(1), 90–98.

14. Le Phuoc, D., Hauswirth, M. (2009). Linked Open Data in Sensor Data Mashups. In *Proceedings of the 2nd International Workshop on Semantic Sensor Networks, CEUR*.
15. Lee, B. T., Chen, Y., Chilton, L., Connolly, D., Dhanaraj, R., Hol-lenbach, J., et al. (2006). Exploring and analyzing linked data on the semantic web. In *Proceedings of the 3rd International Semantic Web User Interaction Workshop (SWUI06)* (pp. 06).
16. Leontiadis, I., Efstratiou, C., Mascolo, C., & Crowcrof, Jt. (2012). SenShare: transforming sensor networks into multi-application sensing infrastructures. In G. P. Picco & W. Heinzelman (Eds.), *Proceedings of the 9th European conference on Wireless Sensor Networks (EWSN'12)* (pp. 65–81). Berlin, Heidelberg: Springer-Verlag.(Ed.), *Proceedings of the 9th European conference on Wireless Sensor Networks* (pp. 65–81). Berlin, Heidelberg: Springer-Verlag.
17. Mayer, S. (2010). Deployment and mashup creation support for smart things, Institute for Pervasive Computing Department of Computer Science ETH Zurich. Last access April 2013, http://www.vladtrifa.com/files/publications/Mayer10.pdf.
18. OMA. (2012). Open Mashup Alliance for Enterprise Mashups. Last access April 2013, www.openmashup.org/.
19. Page, K., Roure, D., David, C., Martinez, K., Sadler, J., & Kit, O. Y. (2009). Linked sensor data: RESTfully serving RDF and GML. In *International Workshop on Semantic Sensor Networks* (pp. 49–63, vol. 522).
20. Patni, H., Henson, C., Cooney, M., Sheth, A., & Thirunarayan, K. (2011). Demonstration: real-time semantic analysis of sensor streams. In *Semantic Sensor Networks, 2011* (pp. 108).
21. Pautasso, C., Zimmermann, O., & Leymann, F. (2008). RESTful web services versus big web services: making the right architectural decision. In *Proceeding of the 17th International Conference on World Wide Web*. Last access April 2013, http://portal.acm.org/citation.cfm?id=1367606.
22. Priyantha, N., et al. (2008). Tiny web services: design and implementation of interoperable and evolvable sensor networks. In *Proceedings of the 6th ACM Conference on Embedded Network Sensor Systems*. USA.
23. RDF Query Language, Last access April 2013, http://139.91.183.30:9090/RDF/RQL/.
24. Resource Description Framework (RDF). (2010). Last access April 2013, http://www.w3.org/RDF/.
25. RFC 2068. (1997). Hypertext Transfer Protocol - HTTP/1.1. Last access April 2013, http://tools.ietf.org/html/rfc2068.
26. RFC 2616. (1999). Hypertext Transfer Protocol - HTTP/1.1. Last access April 2013, http://tools.ietf.org/html/rfc2616.
27. RFC 4944. (2007). Transmission of IPv6 packets over IEEE 802.15.4 networks, IETF. Last access April 2013, http://tools.ietf.org/html/rfc4944.
28. RFC 5785. (2010). Defining well-known uniform resource identifiers (URIs). Last access April 2013, http://tools.ietf.org/html/rfc5785.
29. Richardson L., & Ruby, S. (2008). *RESTful web services* (pp. 79–105). OReilly Media, cap. 4.
30. Schor, L., Sommer, P., & Wattenhofer, R. (2009). Towards a zero-configuration wireless sensor network architecture for smart buildings. In *BuildSys '09: Proceedings of the First ACM Workshop on Embedded Sensing Systems for Energy-Efficiency in, Buildings* (pp. 31–36).
31. Silva, J. M., Rahman, A. S., & El Saddik, A. (2008). Web 3.0: a vision for bridging the gap between real and virtual. In *1st ACM International Workshop on Communicability Design and Evaluation in Cultural and Ecological Multimedia System*. Vancouver British Columbia, Canada.
32. SPARQL Query Language for RDF. (2008). http://www.w3.org/TR/rdf-sparql-query/.
33. Sun SPOT World. (2011). Last access April 2013, http://www.sunspotworld.com/.
34. Trifa, V., Wiel S.; Guinard, D., & Bohnert, T. (2009). Design and implementation of a gateway for web-based interaction and management of embedded devices. Last access April 2013, http://citeseerx.ist.psu.edu/viewdoc/summary?doi=10.1.1.155.4806.
35. Wu, F., Kao, Y., & Tseng, Y. (August 2011). From wireless sensor networks towards cyber physical systems. *Pervasive and Mobile Computing, 7*(4), 397–413, ISSN 1574–11.
36. XML. Extensible Markup Language Specification. Last access April 2013, http://www.w3.org/TR/xml/.

Chapter 4
The Sensor Integration Module (SIM)

Abstract The SmartSensor architecture encompasses three main software modules: (i) the *Sensor Integration Module* (SIM), (ii) the *Programming and Execution Module* (PEM), and (iii) the *Web 3.0 Integration Module* (WIM). In this Chapter we detail the SIM logical and physical components as well as their operation. In the SmartSensor infrastructure a set of wireless sensor networks (WSN) is connected to the Web through one gateway node, that exposes to client applications the sensing data produced by the networks as RESTful Web resources. The Sensor Integration Module (SIM) is responsible for providing the RESTful interface to access the resources of a given WSN. Its components receive application requests describing their desired sensing data, translate HTTP messages to and from the several sensor specific formats and protocols, coordinate the functions needed to meet the received sensing tasks and manage the different communication models required to produce and deliver the data back to the requesting applications.

Keywords Web of Things (WoT) · REST · HTTP · XML · JSON · Wireless sensor networks · Integrating WSN · Restful services

4.1 Overview

As previously stated, the SmartSensor project considers a system consisting of a set of wireless sensor networks with technologies/platforms possibly distinct, connected to the Web through one gateway node, and a set of client applications. The WSNs are exposed and their data accessed by applications as Web resources, using the concept of RESTful services. The access to the resources provided by a specific WSN is realized through the Sensor Integration Module (SIM). The following Sections present the SIM logical and physical architecture, describing how its software components are deployed in each type of node that composes the SmartSensor infrastructure. As we discussed, SIM components are deployed in sensor nodes and in gateway nodes.

F. C. Delicato et al., *Middleware Solutions for the Internet of Things*,   29
SpringerBriefs in Computer Science, DOI: 10.1007/978-1-4471-5481-5_4,
© The Author(s) 2013

The current implementation of SmartSensor considers WSN nodes from MEMSIC,[1] Arduino,[2] and SUN SPOT platforms.[3]

4.2 The SIM Logical Architecture

The UML diagrams of Figs. 4.1 and 4.2 illustrate the main components of the SIM logical architecture. The deployment diagram of Fig. 4.1 provides an overview of components for each type of physical node (sensor and gateway) considered in Smart-Sensor. The UML class diagram in Fig. 4.2 details the classes and subclasses that compose the gateway Communication Component.

4.2.1 Gateway Components

As depicted in the diagram of Fig. 4.1, the logical architecture of the gateway node is organized into five software components, described below.

4.2.1.1 Web Interface

This component is the ultimate responsible for providing a uniform Web interface to access the WSN *as a service*. It enables that services provided by the sensor nodes of a

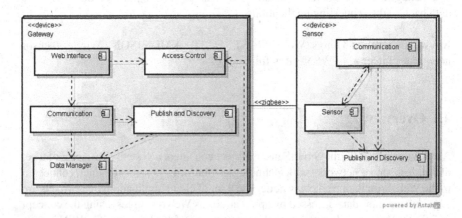

Fig. 4.1 SIM components deployed in the gateway node and in the sensor nodes

---

[1] http://www.memsic.com/

[2] http://www.arduino.cc/

[3] http://www.sunspotworld.com/

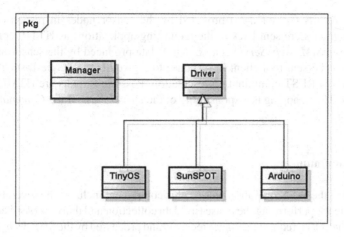

Fig. 4.2 Classes of the communication component

WSN connected to the SmartSensor infrastructure be available in the Web as RESTful resources. Considering the traditional operation phases of a WSN, this component is responsible for phase (ii) submission of application requests (see Sect. 3.2). The main class of this component is called *SIM_Web_Service* and it simply consists of a traditional REST-based Web Service installed in a Web server. *SIM_Web_Service class* handles all the HTTP messages exchanged between client applications and the WSN connected through the respective gateway node.

In order to achieve its goals, the *SIM_Web_Service class* directly interacts with the classes of the *Communication component*. HTTP requests received from applications are processed in the Web server 'as any other request for Web resources. A request message identifies through the URI path (i) a given WSN resource (accessed via the respective driver type), (ii) a specific device (considered as a sub resource of the driver) and (iii) some functionality provided by the device (considered sub resource of the device). Thus, the path of an HTTP request is initially used to identify the type of driver from the device whose service is being requested, then to identify a particular device (if desired) and finally the service (type of sensing data) provided by this device. For example, in the path /spotApi/spot-0f40/temperature, the first part "/spotApi" identifies the driver for this type of device (indicating that it is a Sun SPOT platform sensor). The second part "/device-0f40" identifies the specific node (SPOT), where "0f40" is the last four digits of the SPOT MAC address. Finally, the part "/temperature" is used to identify the temperature sensing unit of the respective SPOT. After analysing the content (body and header) of the HTTP request message, the description of the required sensing task needs to be extracted from the message and forwarded to the sensor nodes able to attend such request. The *Manager class* of the *Communication component* is responsible for determining the nodes that are able to perform a received sensing task. Therefore, after processing an HTTP request message, the *SIM_Web_Service class* reports its content to such component.

Likewise, results (sensor data) provided by the sensor nodes in response to the received requests are sent back to the requesting applications as HTTP reply messages via the *SIM_Web_Service class*. When data produced by the sensor nodes in a WSN is to be sent to a client in response to a given HTTP request, such data is mapped into a REST compliant representation. Possible formats are HTML, XML and JSON. This mapping is responsibility of the *Driver class* of the *Communication component*.

4.2.1.2 Communication

Considering the WSN operation phases, this component includes the several classes responsible for performing the phase (iii) data collection and delivery (see Sect. 3.2).

From the HTTP request messages received and processed by the *SIM_Web_Service class*, this component manages and distributes sensing tasks to the respective sensor nodes, collects the received results and forwards them back to the Web server so that they are properly delivered to the requesting application.

The Manager Class. The *Manager class* of the *Communication component* directly interacts with the *SIM_Web_Service class* and determine, based on the analysis of the incoming messages content and by querying the database maintained at the gateway, which nodes are able to meet the received request (Fig. 4.3). The main parameters used to perform the matching between a requested sensing task and the nodes in a given WSN that are able to execute the task are (i) types of environmental variables to be monitored (depend on the sensing units available in the node); (ii) geographical location of the node; and optionally (iii) quality of service (QoS)

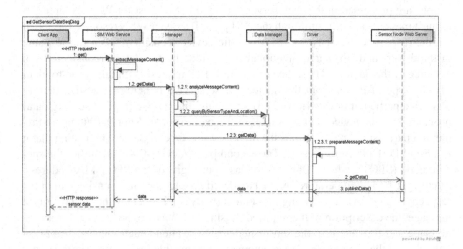

Fig. 4.3 Simplified view of the interactions for the submission of application request messages; message processing; and sensor data delivery

requirements as, for instance, the minimum data accuracy provided by the node, the maximum delay delivered by the network, the maximum lifetime of the node, among others. Upon determining which sensor nodes are used to execute the required sensing task, the *Manager class* is able to know the respective sensor platform(s) to be used to meet the request. Thus, the request message is forwarded to the respective *Driver class* to be translated to the proper data format. After the required sensing task is performed by the WSN and the required sensing data is collected by the nodes, the respective *Driver class* sends to the *Manager class* the translated reply messages directly received from the tasked sensor nodes. The Manager then forwards the message to the *Web Interface component* so that the results of the HTTP request are presented/delivered to the user/client application. The other functionality of the *Manager class* is to determine the type of communication to be used (synchronous or asynchronous) in the message exchange between the gateway and the WSN. Such type is defined from the data delivery model required by the client application.

According to the data delivery model, WSNs can be typically classified in three types: periodic, event-driven and initiated-by-the-observer (or simply request-reply model). In the periodic model, sensor nodes sense and send their collected data continuously, at a predefined rate. In the event-driven model, sensors continuously sense the monitored environment but report information only if an event of interest for the application occurs. In the request-reply model, sensor nodes report their data in response to a synchronous query issued by the application. In this last case, the application is interested in getting a snapshot of values of the monitored phenomenon.

For event-based applications, asynchronous communication is required, for instance, based on the Publish-Subscribe model. The current architecture of Smart-Sensor does not support this model. With such model, a client application registers for events of interest only once and receives new sensor measurements upon the occurrence of an event. The HTTP protocol typically operates in the pull mode, where clients send a request message whenever they need a resource from a Web server. HTTP does not natively provide an event notification mechanism (push mode). A usual way of implementing the push mode would be to repeatedly send an HTTP request message (for instance containing a conditional GET operation) describing the event of interest; whenever the event occurs the reply message body will include the event description; otherwise the message body will be empty. This implementation based on sending repeated requests makes costly the communication for this type of data delivery model. To overcome such drawback, a possible solution would be to modify the original HTTP protocol implementation. One example of such a solution is the TinyREST protocol [5], proposed as part of a joint R&D project between Samsung Advanced Institute of Technology and Fraunhofer FOKUS. TinyREST is a protocol specific to the TinyOS sensor platform that was built based on the REST architecture and principles. The TinyREST implementation provides the clients with the ability to issue HTTP-like messages to accessing MICA [3] motes in a WSN. Besides the standard POST and GET HTTP operations, TinyREST includes a SUBSCRIBE request message. By issuing a SUBSCRIBE message, clients are able to register their interest to specific services provided by sensors/actuators, besides defining personalized parameters depending on the clients needs. Each subscribed client will automatically be notified with a NOTIFY message whenever a desired event has been detected (e.g. a temperature value passing a specified threshold).

Although providing an efficient way for handling event-based applications and asynchronous communication in a WoT connected WSN, the solution offered by TinyREST actually changes the standard HTTP API and implementation. For a WoT solution that needs to be fully compliant to the REST principles, as is the goal of the SmartSensor framework, this is not a suitable option.

Other options involve introducing a third party component to mediate HTTP messages sent by applications to the gateway. An example of such a solution is the Pubsubhubbub protocol.[4] This protocol enables the communication between client and server using a Publish-Subscribe model by employing a component, called Hub, that registers clients (Subscribers) interested in receiving events (about sensor generated data), gets new data provided by the server (the gateway, acting as a Publisher), and deliver data to the respective clients. The SmartSensor designers consider that handling asynchronous communication in Web-enabled WSNs is still an open issue that requires further investigations to be implemented in an efficient and interoperable way.

A periodic data delivery model is implemented in SmartSensor by the submission of a sensing task that describes the desired data type and the frequency of data delivery (data sensing/sending rate). It requires that the user (or application) access the SIM to check the latest data collected by the network. The SIM database is periodically updated with the latest data sent by the sensors, with the frequency previously configured in the nodes. To access the collected data, the user must access the URI: GATEWAY/gateway/rest/getdata/data type.

Such request will return all sensor data of the required type that were collected and stored in the SIM database until the moment of the request. If the user is accessing SmartSensor via PEM, there is the option to automatically refresh the application, which can be configured according to the required frequency, avoiding the need for the user need to resubmit the request or manually update the HTML page where the data is being displayed.

The Driver Class. Another important class of the *Communication component* is the *Driver class*, a super-class that represents the interaction with the sensors from each specific WSN platform to be integrated in the SmartSensor infrastructure. Drivers translate messages and commands to the specific language/protocols of the WSN and vice-versa. This class is extended by subclasses for each sensor platform. As we have already stated, SmartSensor currently provides drivers for the Arduino,[5] SUN SPOT[6] and TinyOS[7] sensor platforms.

The main operations provided by the *Driver class*, regardless of the sensor platform used are described as follows. The advertiseService operation is responsible for handling the advertisement messages (RequestAdvertiseMessage) sent by the gate-

[4] http://pubsubhubbub.googlecode.com/svn/trunk/pubsubhubbub-core-0.3.html

[5] http://www.arduino.cc/

[6] http://www.sunspotworld.com/

[7] http://www.tinyos.net/

way for devices that interact with the respective driver. These messages are generated by classes of the *Publish and Discovery component* and should be sent to the sensors, which respond with a message (AdvertiseMessage) advertising their services, residual energy, among other relevant information. The getData operation is used to task the sensor nodes to collect the sensing data as requested by the client application, according to the desired data delivered model. The publishData operation is responsible for receiving data messages sent by the sensors (containing the collected sensing data).

4.2.1.3 Publish and Discovery

There are two levels of service discovery in a WSN: internal and external (phase (i) of the networks operation, as described in the Chap. 3), and both are implemented by classes from the *Publish and Discovery component*.

The internal discovery enables that sink/gateway nodes know the capabilities of all sensor nodes that compose a given WSN connected to the gateway. In order to implement this feature, in the SmarSensor infrastructure a special message, called AdvertiseMessage, was defined to allow sensor nodes to advertise their capabilities. Such message include the node (local) identifier, a timestamp, the types of sensing units available in the node, geographic location, residual energy, maximum data accuracy/precision provided; supported data rates, supported aggregation functions and supported duty cycles. Advertising messages are sent by a sensor node (i) at the node initialization (upon the network deployment in the target area), (ii) when a new sensor joins a pre-deployed network, and (iii) from time to time, either as a keep alive message sent with a predefined periodicity or upon request by the gateway (via a RequestAdvertiseMessage). Such periodic sent of advertising messages is required given the dynamic nature of the WSN environment, where sensors may be damaged, moved, have their energy depleted, thus no longer participating from the network infrastructure. In SmartSensor, if a connected device does not respond to three consecutive RequestAdvertiseMessage sent by a gateway, such device is considered unreachable and should be removed from the list of devices maintained in the database. AdvertiseMessage messages are disseminated throughout the network by using the communication/routing protocols available at the nodes, until they reach the gateway node. In the gateway, the content of such messages is extracted and stored in a database containing data for the respective WSN connected to the gateway. Gateways are organized in a logical hierarchy and interact among themselves in order to exchange data from their respective WSNs. PEM components execute in the gateways positioned in the highest level of the hierarchy. While gateways at the lower levels only keep information on their respective WSNs, the higher level gateways keep a database with updated information on all networks connected to the SmartSensor infrastructure.

The external service discovery is used by client applications to discover which WSNs provide the services they require, and how to access such services. This is a traditional phase of service discovery according to the Web Services technologies.

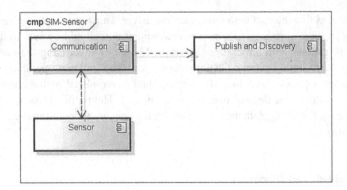

Fig. 4.4 Logical components of sensor nodes

For REST-based Web services, the discovery and navigation through available resources are performed by using URIs. SmartSensor infrastructure provides a REST-based discovery service available through a URI exposed by the Programming and Execution Module (PEM).

4.2.1.4 Access Control

This component includes classes with basic functions (authentication and authorization) for managing the access constraints to the services provided by a given WSN (accessed through a gateway node). Policies are enforced over resource publication and sensing task allocation according to criteria set by network administrators.

4.2.1.5 Data Manager

This component is responsible for storing data in a local database maintained by the gateway. The classes of this component manage the reading and writing operations of the tables responsible for storing sensing data as well as all the information (metadata) about sensing capabilities offered by each network node in the WSN connected to the respective gateway.

4.2.2 Sensor Node Components

Figure 4.4 shows the SIM main software components that should be deployed in the sensor nodes. The components are described as follows.

4.2.2.1 Communication

As we previously mentioned, WoT employs REST principles to expose the services of smart devices available on the Web by using two different approaches. In the first approach, an embedded HTTP server is deployed directly on the devices and the functionality of these devices is provided as RESTful resources. The second approach is adopted whenever a device does not have hardware resources enough to run an embedded server, or when it is not necessary that such device is directly accessed via Web. For these cases, another, more powerful device can be used as a bridge to expose the services provided by the constrained device via a RESTful interface. Such device consists of a WoT gateway. In the SmartSensor project both approaches were implemented. However, as mentioned, independently of either having a server embedded in the sensors or not, the gateway is always used for mediating the interaction of WSNs with the Internet (for the purposes of converting the adopted protocol stacks).

For the first approach, an embedded Web server is directly implemented on each sensor node making it an autonomous and Web-enabled device. The use of servers embedded in physical objects enables the functionality of these objects to be available as Web resources. However, the technologies used in the creation of traditional Web services are not designed to be used on devices that are severe restricted in resources and battery powered (eg, wireless sensors) [4]. Therefore, so that Web servers are used in embedded devices, they must meet a number of requirements. In Ref. [4] a set of requirements and standards for the implementation of embedded servers were presented. An example of a requirement to be met in a standardized way is the compression of HTTP protocol messages [1]. For the definition of a generic architecture for embedded servers, the SmartSensor project followed a bottom-up approach, in which such an architecture was derived from an existing implementation of a embedded server deployed in a specific sensor platform, the SUN Spot. The implementation used as a reference for the SmartSensor design is described in the WebOfThings project.[8] From the analysis of the components of this existing architecture, a platform-independent generalization was performed and adopted in the SmartSensor logical architecture to guide the possible implementation of a server embedded in other sensor platforms.

The embedded Web server is basically a very lean version of an HTTP server, capable of handling HTTP request messages and generating reply messages server. Thus, it natively supports the four main operations of the HTTP protocol (GET, POST, PUT, DELETE, i.e the verbs of REST). In this case, the *Communication component* in the sensor nodes encompasses the typical classes of an HTTP engine, including a request dispatcher and a response builder [2].

For the second approach, the *Communication component* includes the classes and interfaces native for each sensor platform, which are responsible for the communication tasks. Such classes should participate in the completion of three tasks: (i) sending messages advertising the capabilities of the device; (ii) receiving

---

[8] http://www.webofthings.org/projects/

messages requesting for a given sensing task/data, and (iii) sending reply messages in response to request messages (after the required sensing tasks have been performed).

4.2.2.2 Sensor

This component includes classes responsible for keeping the current state of the sensor nodes, both regarding the available resources, such as residual energy, and the acquired sensing data. As the data collected by the sensing units are not always immediately transmitted (depending on the data delivery model required by the application and also on the adopted data aggregation intervals), the classes of this component shall keep the data in the node memory until they are processed and sent through the network towards the gateway.

4.2.2.3 Publish and Discovery

The classes of this component are responsible for implementing the internal discovery service. Therefore, a class is required to create messages advertising the node features and send these messages whenever required. Classes of the Publish-Discovery and the *Sensor components* directly depend on the low-level primitives provided by the sensor operation system.

4.2.3 The SIM Physical Architecture

The logical architecture previously described for SIM was instantiated on a gateway node implemented in Java and on sensor nodes from three different technologies: Mica platform/TinyOS, Arduino and Sun Spot. In the next subsections we describe the gateway physical architecture and the components for the MICA/TinyOS platform. Description of the components implemented for Arduino and Sun Spot platforms are outside the scope of the Book.

4.2.3.1 WoT Gateway

Despite the REST principles are suitable for the integration of physical devices to the WoT, such devices do not always have sufficient computational resources to support an embedded server. Therefore, the direct integration of real-world devices with the Web is still a complex task, especially in cases of extremely limited resources devices such as the sensor nodes in a WSN. In such cases, a different strategy for the integration should be adopted, based on the utilization of an intermediate device, Smart Gateway or WoT gateway. Smart Gateways have two basic functions: to expose a RESTful interface via URIs that identify and provide access to physical objects (smart devices) and their resources, and to realize the communication with physical objects using their provided APIs. In other words, the Smart Gateway acts as a bridge between the Web and smart devices, by providing a RESTful Web interface to access resources and sub resources provided by these devices and communicate with them through their specific APIs. The gateway node plays the role of an interface between client applications and WSNs connected to the WoT, serving as the entry point for the submission of application requests and as a concentrator for data sent by the sensor nodes.

In the SmartSensor architecture, a gateway node is a synonymous of a sink node, and its functionalities are partially implemented in a computer (a PC running Debian GNU/Linux i386 in the project) and partly on wireless communication modules that are dependent on the different radio technologies used in WSNs. All the WSN platforms used in the SmartSensor project adopt variations of the ZigBee protocol [3]; therefore the sink/gateway wireless module implements this protocol to enable the communication with sensors.

Each Smart Gateway has an IP address, runs an HTTP server and includes several drivers, each one responsible for translating to/from proprietary protocols of the different WSN technologies connected to the infrastructure. Thus, all Web requests sent to a sensor node through the provided RESTful API are mapped by the gateway to a request in the proprietary WSN API and transmitted to the respective node by using the communication protocol understood by the device (for example, the Zigbee protocol).

The classes and components described for the SIM logical architecture were implemented in the Java programing language. For the Gateway Web Server, the Apache Tomcat version 6.0.33 was used and Apache Derby relational database was adopted as the Gateway Database. The *Data Manager component* is responsible for data storage and management in the Gateway Database and its mains class is the *DataDB class*. DataDB is a typical persistency class, mediating all the read and write operations performed in the two main tables kept in the gateway. The Data_Read table is responsible for the storage of the sensor generated data, while the Services table contains the list of capabilities offered by each node in a given WSN.

4.2.3.2 MICA/TinyOS Sensor Plataforms

MICA motes are the category of sensor nodes manufactured by MEMSIC (formerly Crossbow). MEMSIC technology for WSN platforms is based on the TinyOS operating system and programs to be deployed in the nodes are written in nesC language. As specified in the MIS logical architecture, a sensor node must have three basic functional blocks to be integrated into the SmartSensor infrastructure: Communication, Publication, and Sensor. TinyOS adopts a component-based and event-driven programing model, and nesC is a language derived from C, so it does not natively incorporate concepts of object-oriented programing. The main units of programming in TinyOS environment are components and interfaces. Therefore, in order to implement the functionalities of the three logical blocks defined for the sensors three

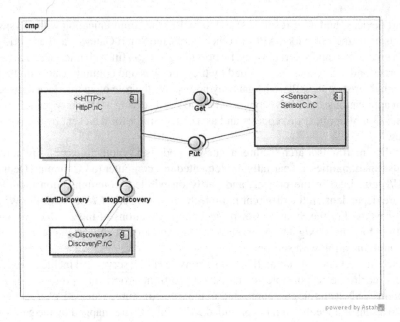

Fig. 4.5 Components e interfaces of sensor nodes in the TinyOS platform

major components and their respective interfaces were created. Such components and interfaces are illustrated in the diagrams of Fig. 4.5, and briefly described below.

In the version implemented for the Mica/TinyOS platform, the approach adopted for the integration in the WoT was based in the implementation of an HTTP server embedded in the sensor nodes. Therefore, for such WSN platform, the *Communication component* includes classes responsible for receiving and processing HTTP request messages, and then for composing and sending the respective HTTP reply messages. The features of the *Sensor component* are realized by software components already existing in the sensor platform; it was not necessary to implement them. However, the implementation of the *Publish-Discovery classes* was hampered by the available node interfaces. The access to the node state information on Mica platform is restricted to the sensed data, and there is no API to report, for example, the residual energy of the sensor. Information such as the maximum precision provided by a given sensing unit comes preconfigured from the factory, and there is no native method to get/set such an information. Data such as the node geographic location is only available either if the node is endowed with a GPS unit or if some algorithm for node location is employed. Therefore, in the current version of the SmartSensor infrastructure all the relevant metadata for sensor nodes from the Mica/TinyOS platform was statically configured as parameters in the advertising messages sent by the nodes.

The main software components implemented for the Mica/TinyOS sensor nodes are showed in Fig. 4.5 and briefly described below:

- *SensorC*: this component is deployed in each sensor node to implement the communication based on the interfaces provided by HttpP.
- *HttpP*: this component implements the HTTP protocol API, providing RESTful interfaces for communication with the gateway node (and also between the sensor nodes themselves).
- *DiscoveryP*: this is the component responsible for the (internal) publication and discovery of the capabilities of sensor nodes.

In addition to the components of the sensor node, a component is necessary to connect the WSN (based on TinyOS/nesC) to the gateway (in Java). This component is baseC, implemented in nesC, and responsible for making the connection with the Gateway Web Server through a serial communication interface.

4.2.3.3 Operation

As previously mentioned, a WSN integrated to the WoT works according to three phases: (i) internal and external service discovery, (ii) submission of sensing tasks, (iii) data collection and delivery. Except for the external discovery phase, which is totally the responsibility of the gateway, the other phases are implemented by the sensor node components previously described. During the internal service discovery phase an HTTP PUT message is used to advertise the sensing capabilities of each node to the gateway, thus respecting the RESTful principles to maintain a uniform interface for accessing all data (and metadata) from the connected sensors.

Phases (ii) and (iii) of the network operation are illustrated in the UML activity diagram of Fig. 4.6. In the diagram, the Client swimming lane represents the client side of an HTTP-based interaction with a Web Server. The Gateway Web Server remains listening in a well-known port and waiting to receive a request from client applications, which may be requests for changing some parameters of the sensor (PUT operation) or requests for some monitoring data collected by the sensor (GET operation). In both cases, the received request messages are sent for analysis and subsequent forwarding to the destination sensor node(s). Upon arriving at the gateway, the request message header is analysed, and the following cases are possible: if the message is addressed to the sink node itself, it examines if it is either a Get or Put message; otherwise, the error message 405 is returned to the client. If the message is addressed to the client, it is not forwarded to the WSN, being processed within the gateway. If the message is directed neither to the client nor to the Sink node, a 404 error message is returned to the client. Otherwise, the message is redirected to the specified sensor, group of sensors or broadcasted in the whole network.

Upon the arrival of a message in a sensor node, the message header is analysed, and the following options are possible: if the message is addressed to the sensor itself, it checks whether it is a Get or Put message, if is not either type a 405 error

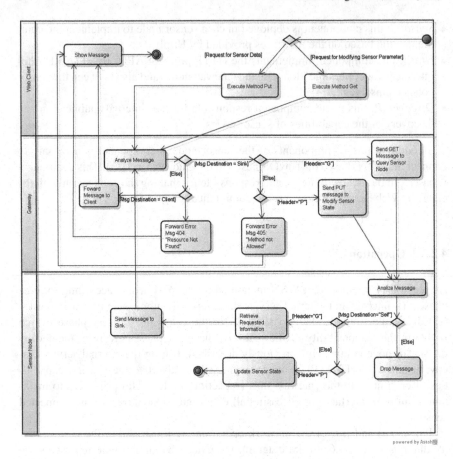

Fig. 4.6 Realization of phases for submission of sensing tasks, data collection and delivery

message is returned. If it is a Get message, the sensor produces a reply message with a copy of the requested information and returns it to the Sink node, which will forward it to the client. If it is a Put message, the sensor will change the current configuration parameter (for example, data sensing or sending rate) according to the values contained in the message.

References

1. Chopan—Compressed HTTP Over PANs (draft-frank-6lowpan-chopan-00). http://w3-org. 9356.n7.nabble.com/Chopan-Compressed-HTTP-Over-PANs-draft-frank-6lowpan-chopan-00-td104660.html. Last access April 2013
2. Guinard, D., Trifa, V., Pham, T., & Liechti, O. (2009). Towards physical mashups in the web of things. *Proceedings of IEEE Sixth International Conference on Networked Sensing Systems.* Pittsburgh, USA

3. MEMSIC solutions. http://www.memsic.com/products/wireless-sensor-networks.html
4. Shelby, Z. (2010). Embedded web services. *IEEE Em Wireless Communications, 17,* 52–57.
5. Luckenbach, T., Gober, P., Arbanowski, S., Kotsopoulos, A., & Kim, K. (2005). TinyREST—a protocol for integrating sensor networks into the internet. *Proceedings of REALWSN 2005*

Chapter 5
The Programming and Execution Module (PEM)

Abstract This Chapter presents the Programming and Execution Module (PEM) of SmartSensor. The main purpose of PEM is to allow end users to program Web mashup applications through the composition of a mixing of public available services and services provided by SmartSensor registered in SIMs. Web mashups are ad-hoc Web applications built upon the combination of real-time information (data, presentation and functionality) from multiple Web sources. The PEM's programming environment provides a Web Mashup DSL (Domain Specific Language) specifically tailored for the WSN environment, as well as an interpreter for such DSL. Moreover, this module contains components for publishing and discovering the capacities of available WSNs. PEM's DSL is an extension of the Enterprise Mashup Markup Language (EMML), which is an open language specification, promoted by the Open Mashup Alliance. The main goals of EMML are to provide programming mechanisms to promote mashup design portability and interoperability of mashup solutions aiming at reducing vendor lock-in.

Keywords Internet of Things (IoT) · Web of Things (WoT) · REST · Applications for IoT · Mashups · EMML · Domain specific language (DSL)

5.1 Overview

The SmartSensor project considers a system consisting of a set of Wireless Sensor Networks (WSN) with technologies/platforms possibly distinct, connected to the Web through one gateway node, and a set of client applications. The WSNs are exposed and their data accessed by applications as Web resources, using the concept of RESTful services. Such approach allows building several types of value-added applications on top of loosely coupled services provided by physical devices and other Web resources, which can be easily shared and reused. The resources are decoupled to the concrete implementation of services and therefore they can be arbitrarily represented by means of various formats, such as XML or JSON. An appealing type of application made available through the SmartSensor consists in Web mashups. Web mashups are ad-hoc Web applications built upon the combination of real-time information (data, presentation and functionality) from multiple Web sources.

The goal of the Programming and Execution Module (PEM) of SmartSensor is to allow end users to program Web mashup applications through the composition of a mixing of public available services and services provided by SmartSensor registered SIMs. The PEM's programming environment provides a DSL (Domain Specific Language) specifically tailored for the WSN environment, as well as an interpreter for such DSL. PEM's DSL is an extension of the Enterprise Mashup Markup Language (EMML). EMML is an open language specification promoted by the Open Mashup Alliance (OMA) [3, 4].

Section 5.1 explaining the concept and the technologies associated with the creation of mashup applications, showing their main features along with examples of companies that have successfully used such approach. Next Sect. 5.2 we describe the architecture and main features of the Programming and Execution Module.

5.2 Web Mashups

Web Mashups are ad-hoc Web applications built upon the combination of real-time information (data, presentation and functionality) from multiple Web sources. The term *Web Mashup* implies easy, fast integration, frequently using open application programming interfaces (API) and data sources to produce augmented results that were not necessarily the original reason for producing the raw data [4, 5]. Data and presentation information typically comes in formats such as Rich Site Summary (RSS) or Atom feeds, different XML based formats, or as HTML, or other graphical elements. Application functionality can come from any Web accessible API as, for example, a JavaScript code. Different technologies such as PHP, Ruby, or Java can be used to combine data, functionality, and presentation to create the Mashup applications [1, 6].

Developers are currently creating a plethora of mashups covering a wide range of domains, from esoteric mashups that record the location and availability of rare gaming consoles to those that create Sudoku games from Flickr photos. However, there are also more generally useful mashups, such as those offering weather information and mapping services.

For enterprises, the Web mashup paradigm can be used as a simple and cheap way to access data and combine different data sources, encouraging innovation by allowing new ideas to be tested, refined and improved at very low cost. One of the first organizations to leverage mashup technology for immediate results was the JP Morgan Chase [3]. This company employed a rudimentary mashup technology to integrate real-time data on commodity performance within analytical tools that allowed security traders to monitor up to 500 portfolios at once. This mashup was named Trading Algorithm Optimizer (TAO) [3]. Another example of Web applications built using mashup technology integrates Google maps with environmental data from the Brazilian National Institute for Space Research (INPE). This application displays, in real time, places within the Brazilian Amazon forest with occurrences of fire and deforestation [2]. The reader can refer to Web directories and marketplaces like ProgrammableWeb.com, StrikeIron.com and Mashable.com to find other live examples.

At a first glance, it is not easy to identify the differences between mashups and traditional forms of integration. In this context, the work of Benatallah, Casati, and Daniel [1] provides useful insights to identify mashup development specificities. They say that a key point to understand such differences is to contrast de focus of both approaches. On one hand, Mashups focus on opportunistic integration, occurring on the Web targeted to user's personal use and for nonbusiness critical applications. On the other hand, traditional composition (for example, workflow based business compositions) focuses on well-defined and repeatable enterprise processes. Moreover, enterprise processes have, besides the functional requirements, a set of system wide requirements (for instance, scalability and security) that are not present in most of today mashup applications. The implementation of system wide requirements makes the overall development of enterprises process rather complex. Mashup employs an end-user oriented development that requires improved tool support with strong reuse of software components to allow end-users to easily compose their own mashups. Therefore, integration paradigms focused on end-users are needed for allowing easy and simple discovery and integration of mashups.

5.3 SmartSensor Programming and Execution Module

The main purpose of the Programming and Execution Module (PEM) is to allow end users to program Web mashup applications through the composition of a mixing of public available services and services provided by SmartSensor registered in SIMs. The PEM's programming environment provides a DSL (Domain Specific Language) specifically tailored for the WSN environment, as well as an interpreter for such DSL. Moreover, this module contains components for publishing and discovering the capacities of available WSNs.

PEM's DSL is an extension of the Enterprise Mashup Markup Language (EMML). EMML is an open language specification promoted by the Open Mashup Alliance (OMA) [3, 4]. The main goals of EMML are to provide programming mechanisms to promote mashup design portability and interoperability of mashup solutions aiming at reducing vendor lock-in. EMML allows the composition of mashups with traditional services in the Web (i.e. services based on SOAP, REST, third party APIs, and SQL databases).

Figure 5.1 shows the main components of the PEM: (i) Publishing and Discovery; (ii) Data Manager; and (iii) EMML Script Manager.

The *Publishing and Discovery component* is responsible for finding out the WSNs that provide the services required by a mashup application and how to access such

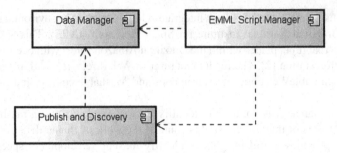

Fig. 5.1 PEM components

services. This component relies on the *SIM Web interface component* to provide information about sensing capacities of registered WSNs. For doing so, the *SIM Web interface component* implements a functionality to send advertising messages containing WSN metadata to PEM. A typical advertising message contains the network identifier, types of sensing units in the network, geographic localization, network creation time, RESTful Web Services provided by the network, among other relevant information. These messages are sent whenever a new WSN is registered within SIM, whenever new sensing capacities are deployed in a registered WSN, or whenever SIM detects nonoperating networks, which are no longer part of the infrastructure. After receiving an advertising message, the *Publish and Discovery component* calls the *Data Manager component* to update the information about the registered WSN capabilities.

The *Data Manager component* is responsible for managing all data structures required by PEM.

The *EMML Script Manager component* provides mechanisms to create, interpret, and execute Web mashups specified through EMML scripts. Mashup creation in PEM follows the same model as defined in the EMML specification, described in the next Section.

5.3.1 EMML Programming Model

The EMML language has a number of specific elements that allow the programming of mashups scripts. These elements allow a developer to perform the invocation and consumption of remote data, the processing and enrichment of these data, the programming of the mashup control logic, and the use of databases to manage the handling of such information. The EMML programming elements can be extended using macros. The PEM's EMML script manager uses the macro functionality for creating a domain-specific language (DSL) to facilitate the construction of physical mashups based on information provided by WSN.

Table 5.1 EMML commands

• **Data consumption**	– While
– Invoke	– For
– Direct Invoke	– Foreach
– Input	– Parallel
– Output	– Sequence
• **Data transformation** (*mashup*)	• **Macros**
– Filter	– Macro
– Join	– Include
– Merge	• **Debug**
– Select	
– Group	– Display
• **Data enrichment**	• **Transactions**
– Append	– SQL
– Constructor	– SQL Update
– Annotate	– Begin TX
– Assign	– Commit TX
– Variable	– Rollback TX
• **Operations for control logics and error handling**	• **Meta operations**
– If-else	– Template UserMeta

The capabilities of EMML can be broadly classified into sets of operations, as listed in Table 5.1. The following paragraphs illustrate the operation of some of these EMML programming elements. The complete EMML reference can be found in [4].

The <directinvoke> EMML element is used to invoke and consume diferent types of services such as: HTML, RSS/ATOM, REST and SOAP. The <directinvoke> element supports HTTP verbs GET, POST, PUT, and DELETE. HTTP Header and cookie support is also available, thus providing capability to consume a wide variety of Web services. Figure 5.2 shows an example of the usage of the <directinvoke> element. In this Figure, the endpoint specifies the URL of the service to be consumed; *u* and *f* are the input parameters of the service; and *outputvariable* specifies the variable that will receive the result of the service invocation.

The <filter> element allows filtering a set of nodes in a variable, based on a filter expression. In Fig. 5.3, *inputvariable* provides the data input to the filter; *filter-*

```
1    <directinvoke endpoint="http://weather.yahooapis.com/forecastrss"
2        w="2442047"
3        u="f"
4        outputvariable="result"/>
```

Fig. 5.2 Usage example of <directinvoke> element

```
1        <filter inputvariable="legislators"
2            filterexpr = "/response/legislators/legislator[ gender = 'F' ]"
3            outputvariable="femaleLegislators"/>
4
```

Fig. 5.3 Usage example of <filter> element

```
1    <variables>
2        <variable name="destination" type="document"/>
3        <variable name="local" type="string" default="US"/>
4    </variables>
5    ...
6    <if condition="$destination//country != $local">
7        <directinvoke endpoint="http://weather.yahooapis.com/forecastrss?p=94102"
8            method="get" outputvariable="$sfWeather"/>
9    </if>
```

Fig. 5.4 Usage example of <if> element

expr contains an XPath [7] expression that sets the filter condition; and *outputvariable* defines variable that will receive the output of filter processing.

The *<if>* element is responsible for handling the control structures if-elseif-else in scripts. The elements *<elseif>* and *<else>* are optional. An example of this element is shown in Fig. 5.4.

5.3.2 Extending EMML

The EMML <macro> element allows creating user-defined statements to be used in mashup scripts. Macros are snippets of mashup logic that can accept input parameters and produce output. Macros can be defined within a single mashup or they can be defined in macro libraries so that they can be shared among mashups. The macro functionality is used in PEM to create a mashup domain-specific language (DSL) for WSN. This DSL is implemented as a macro library of PEM that provides additional functionality to manipulate WSM information.

The following macros are currently implemented:

- *ShowRSSFs*: Macro responsible for querying the PEM Data Manager about available WSNs (identification, sensing capabilities, etc.).
- *SortbyData*: Macro that order the data received from WSN sensors by date (ascending or descending order).
- *SortbyDate*: Macro responsible for ordering, in chronological order, the values collected by a sensor of a WSN.
- *FilterSensor*: Macro that filters WSN data according to a given type of sensor (i.e., temperature, light, etc.).
- *FilterPlatform*: Macro that filters WSN data according to a particular platform (i.e. Arduino or TinyOS).

- *JoinRSSF*: Macro responsible for merging into a single XML file values collected by various WSN.
- *CountMacro*: Macro responsible for counting the number of values in given data set.
- *FusionMacro*: Macro that performs data fusion on the values collected by a network.

5.4 Integration of PEM with EMML Interpreters

This section describes the process of integrating the PEM module with tools that interpret the EMML language. In its current specification, PEM allows building Web mashups applications by using both textual EMML interpreters or with tools that provide graphical user interfaces. To build Web mashup applications by employing some graphical tool created for this purpose and using as data source the information collected by the SmartSensor infrastructure, it is necessary to integrate these tools to PEM. The infrastructure can be used in conjunction with any tool based on EMML, and in this Book we will illustrate the integration with Presto,[1] from JackBe company. Presto was chosen because it is a widely used platform and has a very detailed documentation and complete information about the use of the EMML language in creating Web mashup applications both textual as graphical.

Presto is an ideal solution for organizations that need to merge real-time data from multiple systems and empower users to create their own dashboards for decision support to measure, monitor and manage business processes and still meeting corporate security and other management requirements.

Presto is a solution that combines three key elements:

- Real Time Data: by providing direct connection to a number of internal or external systems, Presto provides the latest information no matter where it is.
- Self-Assembly Service: by providing non-technical users with visual tools that are easy to use, Presto empowers such users with the ability of working by themselves, with a minimal involvement from IT personnel. Presto reverses the typical 80/20 rule, leaving the business with 80 % of the work and leaving the burden of security and governance for IT.
- Universal: users can get their information no matter where they are or which technologies they use. Presto offers unaltered applications and dashboards for Web portals, smartphones, tablets, spreadsheets and email.

Presto allows advanced users to assemble applications visually in a matter of minutes or hours. It allows connecting to sources of information in real time for faster access, easy and flexible data, benefiting business users through greater self-sufficiency.

---

[1] http://www.jackbe.com/prestodocs/v3.2/presto-intro/prestoIntro.html

5.4.1 Integration Mechanism: Example of Integrating PEM with Presto

The tools for creating Web mashup applications provide several options for recording data sources such as WS* Web Services, databases, Rest-based Web Services, RSS, etc.. SmartSensor users that wish to integrate the PEM module with some existing EMML graphical tool must select the option to record data sources as REST-based Web Service and log each REST URL provided by PEM that he/she wants to utilize.

Figure 5.5 illustrates the option to register a new "REST Web Service" in the initial screen of Presto. In this tool, once selected the option "REST Web Service", a new screen appears requesting the data from the service to be registered. This screen must be completed once for each PEM Web service to be registered for use in the mashup building.

Figure 5.6 shows an example of a registry of the *getServicesSIM* service provided by PEM. This service lists information of all WSNs registered at SmartSensor.

The information returned by the getServicesSIM service can be observed in the XML document shown in Fig. 5.7.

5.4.2 Creating a Web Mashup Application

Once the desired REST services are registered in Presto, we can use them as data sources to create Web Mashup applications. In Presto, registered services can be combined to build Web Mashups using the "Wires" tool, which is part of the platform and allow users to graphically "wire" services together to form Mashup applications. The "Wires" tool has a set of objects that allows the dynamic creation of EMML

Fig. 5.5 Creating a new "REST web service" in PRESTO

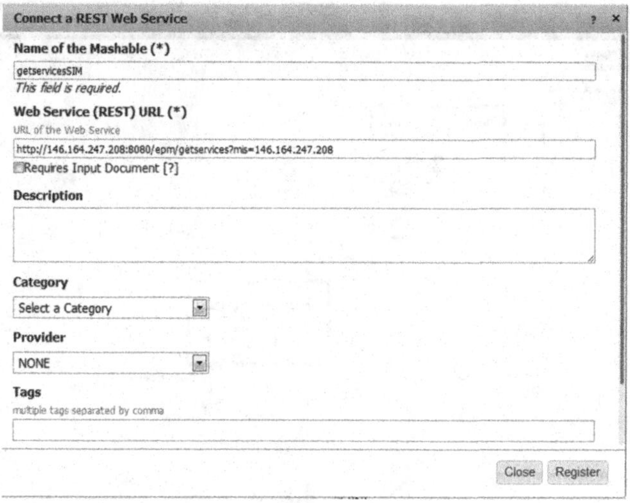

Fig. 5.6 Registering a PEM service in PRESTO

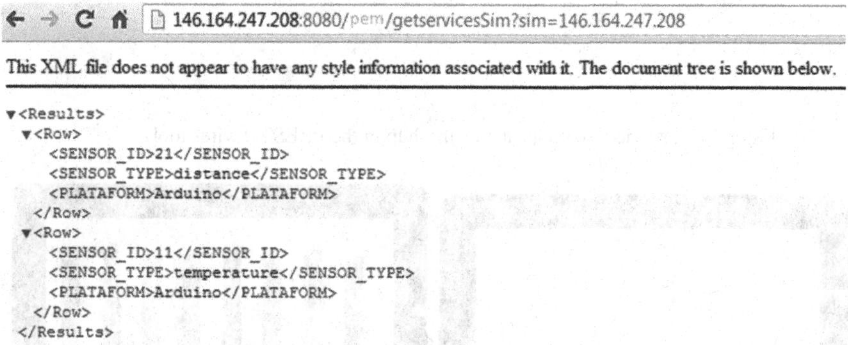

Fig. 5.7 XML document returned by the getServicesSIM service

statements. Wires separates a section for objects that will be used as data sources (the "mashables" section). The previously registered REST Web services are stored in this section.

Figure 5.8 shows an example of two PEM REST services registered as mashable objects in the Presto tool. They are being used to create a Web Mashup application.

Once a Mashup Web application is created, it is possible to select a visual form of presenting it. Figure 5.9 illustrates a Web mashup application that displays historical data collected by sensor of light intensity of a WSN using two different types of presentations.

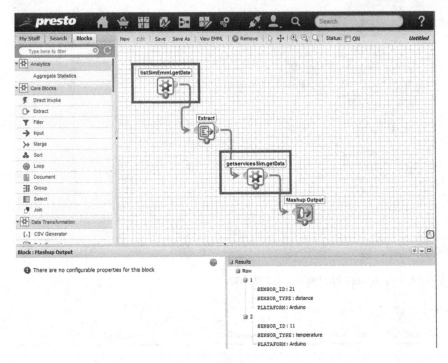

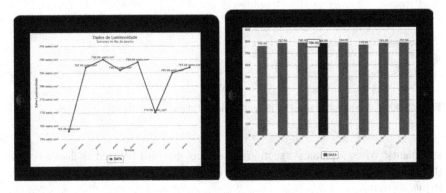

Fig. 5.8 Using PEM services to create a web mashup in the PRESTO wires tool

Fig. 5.9 Two different graphical presentations for the same web mashup data

References

1. Yu, J., Benatallah, B., Casati, F., & Daniel, F. (2008). Understanding mashup development. *IEEE Internet Computing, 12*(5), 44–52.
2. Amazonia.vc Portal. http://www.globoamazonia.com/.

3. Thundian, S. Enterprise Mashup Markup Language (EMML) - Bringing mashups closer to enterprise by susheeb thundian, IT architecture and technology consultant, TCS, whitepaper. http://www.tcs.com/resources/white_papers/Pages/Enterprise-Mashup-Markup-Language-EMML.aspx.
4. Enterprise Mashup Markup Language. (2010). Open mashup alliance. http://www.openmashup.org/.
5. Benslimane, D., Dustdar, S., & Sheth, A. (2008). Services mashups: The new generation of web applications. *IEEE Internet Computing, 12*(5), 13–15.
6. Zang, N., & Rosson, M. B. (2008, September). What's in a mashup? and why? studying the perceptions of web-active end users. In *IEEE Symposium on Visual Languages and Human-Centric Computing. VL/HCC 2008*. (pp. 31–38). IEEE.
7. Skonnard, A., & Gudgin, M. (2001). Essential XML quick reference: A programmer's reference to XML, XPath, XSLT, XML Schema, SOAP, and more. Boston: Addison-Wesley Longman Publishing Co., Inc.

Chapter 6
SmartSensor Proof of Concept

Abstract This chapter illustrates the use of the SmartSensor infrastructure through the development of an application in the domain of smart buildings. Smart buildings are buildings instrumented with smart devices designed to provide high flexibility of use and the ability to evolve and adapt according to the needs of organizations and human beings, aiming at increasing users comfort and safety and optimizing the operation and managing of several functions inside and outside the building while increasing its energy efficiency. There are plenty of applications within the broad domain of smart buildings, varying from applications to control light, humidity and temperature of rooms to fire and intrusion detection. We choose a parking lot management application to present the main functionalities and potential benefits of SmartSensor. The application consists of a wireless sensor network (WSN) based vehicle detection sub-system connected to the SmartSensor infrastructure. The WSN gathers information on the availability of each parking lot and the SmartSensor infrastructure processes the information and provides a Web interface to guide the driver to the available lots.

Keywords Internet of Things (IoT) · Web of Things (WoT) · REST · Applications for IoT · Mashups · EMML · Parking Lot · Smart buildings

6.1 Overview

This chapter demonstrates the use of the SmartSensor infrastructure through the development of an application in the domain of smart buildings. According to [2], smart buildings are buildings equipped with smart devices designed and constructed to offer great flexibility of use, providing the ability to evolve and adapt according to the needs of organizations and to provide at each moment, the best possible support for their activities. Furthermore, smart buildings must be equipped with systems for automation, computing and communications, which enable, in an integrated and

F. C. Delicato et al., *Middleware Solutions for the Internet of Things*,
SpringerBriefs in Computer Science, DOI: 10.1007/978-1-4471-5481-5_6,
© The Author(s) 2013

consistent way, the effective management of the resources available in the building, boosting increases in productivity, allowing energy savings and offering high levels of comfort and safety to the individuals that work in them.

Examples of smart building applications are: temperature, lighting, air quality and windows (natural ventilation) control; applications that monitor and shutdown unattended devices; security applications to protect personnel (access control) and building properties (anti-theft), parking lot management, detection and management of emergency situations, just to name a few. Such applications often monitor physical variables extracted from the target environment, such as light, vibration, temperature, proximity, presence, chemicals (smoke or gas) and electric voltage.

In order to efficiently manage such applications, the notion of integration arises. Integration is defined as the ability to communicate, collaborate and exchange information between applications to achieve common goals [2]. Examples of advantages of integrating applications are: (i) more efficient use of resources, such as energy, computational, and even human resources, (ii) fast and more coordinated responses to monitored physical events, (iii) the ability to correlate information between applications to optimize the decision process, (iv) decision chaining between integrated applications, i.e., a decision made in a given application may trigger another decision on a different application. As an example, in the occurrence of a fire hazard, a service of detection and management of emergency situations needs to interact with many other services such as: lighting, elevators, parking lot, building access control. These services, whenever informed of the existence of a fire in a particular area of the building can trigger actions such as depressurization and smoke removal of the affected area, pressurization of evacuation areas, automatically disabling elevators and moving the occupied cars to safe floors, prevent access to people in general to areas that may be at risk of being affected by the sinister, allow free exit from sinister places, and block access to building and parking areas that may be at risk.

Many smart buildings services require continuous monitoring of various environmental parameters inside and outside the building using sensors and actuators [1, 2]. Moreover, several services demand interaction between sensing data and information systems that manage the operation of the building. Thus, a key requirement for an efficient monitoring and controlling is that all sensors and actuators are addressable over the network to exchange data with corporative intranet or the Internet. In this context, the use of a WoT infrastructure can bring a set of benefits as the enabler technology to achieve the degree of interoperability among senor instrumented spaces in a smart buildings and an internal or external Web-based network. In the next section, we describe the development of a smart building application using the SmartSensor infrastructure.

6.2 Parking Lot Application

In this section, we describe a smart building application that provides guidance to drivers that need to park a car in one of the available parking lots within a given building. A challenge usually found in applications for managing parking lots is to

Fig. 6.1 Schematic draw of
an inductive loop

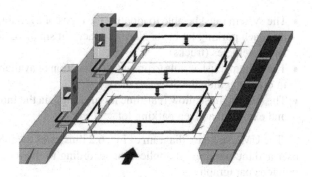

effectively detect vehicles. Many solutions use inductive loops (Fig. 6.1) to tackle
this issue [3]. However, inductive loops have high costs of both installation and
maintenance [4]. In this sense, an easy and cost effective solution option is to use a
WSN. Wireless sensors can be easily deployed in existing parking lots without the
need for excavation and expensive cable installations required by inductive loops.
Moreover, the flexibility to reconfigure sensors already installed, together with the
availability of low cost sensors capable of detecting vehicles, make WSN a natural
candidate to solve the emerging problems of monitoring and control of parking lots
in smart buildings.

Our illustrative application consists of a WSN based vehicle detection sub-system
connected to the SmartSensor infrastructure. WSN gathers information on the availability of each parking lot and the SmartSensor infrastructure processes the information and provides a Web interface to guide the driver to the available parking
lots.

WSNs have great potential to provide an easy and cost effective solution for the
parking lot management application. Its usage along with a WoT solution allows
remote and real-time access to the information on the availability of lots besides
other useful information, thus increasing the efficiency and manageability of large
parking lots, while saving time for the user.

6.2.1 Application Requirements

The Proof of Concept (PoC) parking lot application was developed according to the
following requirements:

- The system must provide a list with the location of all parking lots registered in
  the SmartSensor infrastructure. Such a list must be published as a Web mashup
  application in order to allow end users to easily locate the nearest parking related
  to his/her current location.
- The system must provide information about the number of available spaces in each
  parking lot registered in the system.

- The system must be able to identify the types of available spaces (normal or large) that each parking lot have. Normal spaces fit small vehicles while large spaces fit larger vehicles (trucks).
- The system must be able to provide the location of available spaces within a parking in order to guide the driver to them.
- The system must allow real-time monitoring, via the Internet, of vehicles entrance and exit from a given parking lot.

The UML use case diagram of Fig. 6.2 illustrates the interactions between the end user and the parking lot application according to the requirements described in the previous paragraph.

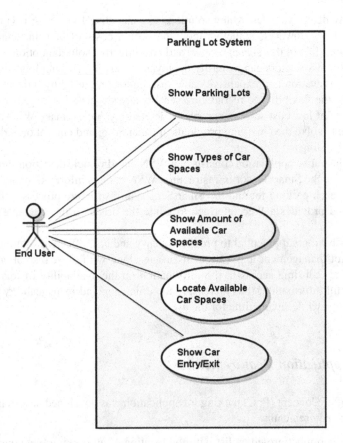

Fig. 6.2 UML use case diagram representing the Parking Lot application

Fig. 6.3 Parking lot image

6.2.2 Environment Setup

The experiment was conducted in three parking lots located at the Center for Mathematical Sciences and Nature (CCMN) in the Federal University of Rio de Janeiro (UFRJ), Brazil. One of these parking lots is illustrated in Fig. 6.3. This parking lot has three rows with 72 places available in each, summing up 216 monitored car spaces.

To detect vehicles and to distinguish them from other objects, such as a person walking through the parking entrance, one pair of sensor nodes endowed with ultrasonic distance detectors were placed at the entrance and exit of each row of the parking lot, as shown in Fig. 6.3. Whenever an object is detected, each pair of sensor nodes sends its collected data to a sink node (Gateway) using a wireless communication channel. A SIM Driver installed in the sink node receives such data, decodes it, and then forwards it to the *SIM Manager component*. Then, the *Manager component* analyses the data and identifies that it must be forwarded to a specific Web service installed in the SIM to further processing. This Web service is responsible for calculating the width of the detected object, and to infer whether it is a car or other type of object. Whenever a car is detected, the Web service accesses the SIM database to update the current number of available car spaces of the parking lot. Regarding the hardware, both the pairs of sensor nodes and the wireless communication module of the sink node consist of Arduino Uno boards endowed with Xbee Shields for wireless communication. The SIM components are installed in a desktop computer and another computer hosts the PEM components. The details of the hardware used for this experiment are found in Sect. 6.2.3.

Figure 6.4 shows a schematic draw of the configuration of the sensor nodes and sink nodes in the parking lot application. A pair of sensor nodes were placed at the

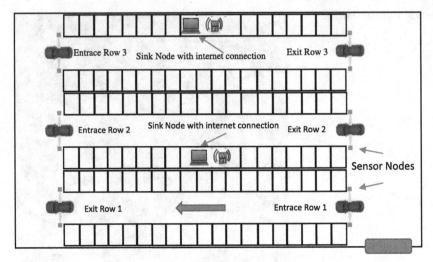

Fig. 6.4 Schematic draw of hardware elements in the parking lot application

entrances and exits of each parking lot row, which is 120 m long and 8 m wide. Two sink nodes were placed in the center of the second and third rows of the parking lot, 60 m away from the entrance of the row. The decision to place the sink node at this location is due to the limitations of radio coverage of the 802.15.4 protocol, implemented by the Zigbee standard [5], which allows data transmission up to a maximum of 100 ft away with direct line-of-sight.

We assume the minimum width of a car as being at least 1.5 m. Therefore, any detected object larger than 1.5 m is considered a car by the application. The pair of sensor nodes at the entrance of each row counts occupied spaces while the par of sensors at the exit of each row counts the vacancy of a space. The sensors of each pair of nodes were placed 8 m apart from each other. To calculate the size of detected objects we use the formula:

$$OS = 8 - DDR - DDL \qquad (6.1)$$

where OS is the size of the object, DDR is the distance measured by the sensor node at the right side, and DDL is the distance measured by the sensor node at the left side. Such formula is applied by the SIM Web service on the measurements sent by the sensor nodes.

6.2.3 Hardware Components

The following hardware components were used to instrument each parking lot:

- 14 Arduino Uno boards: 12 used on sensor nodes and 2 used in the sink nodes;
- 14 Arduino Xbee Shield: 12 used on sensor nodes and 2 used in the sink nodes;
- 12 ultrasonic sensors Maxbotix LV-EZ1;
- 12 batteries;
- 2 laptop computers to host the sink nodes.

Arduino Uno (Fig. 6.5) is a microcontroller board based on the ATmega328 chip, which has 14 digital inputs/outputs pins, 6 analog inputs, a 16 MHz crystal oscilator, a USB connection, a power jack, an ICSP header, and a button reset. The Arduino Uno board can be powered via the USB connection or through an external battery connected its power jack.

Arduino Xbee Shield (Fig. 6.6) can be plugged on top of the Arduino Uno to allow it to communicate wirelessly using Zigbee. It is based on the Xbee module from MaxStream [5]. The Xbee module can communicate up to 30 m indoors or 90 m outdoors (with direct line-of-sight).

Ultrasonic Distance Sensor Maxbotix LV-EZ1 (Fig. 6.7) has a frequency of 42 kHz and reading rate of 20 Hz. The LV-EZ1 has virtually no blind spots, detecting objects up to 6.5 m. The closest measured distance is 15 cm, meaning objects closer than this distance are measured as being 15 cm apart. The ultrasonic distance sensor emits a sound signal that travels up to a solid object, like a wall, and back to the source of the sound. To determine the distance of a solid object, the travel time of the echo is calculated.

The laptops were used to host the SIM components responsible for processing the data collected by the base station and transmit them over the Internet to the PEM. The minimum required configuration is:

Fig. 6.5 Arduino Uno board

Fig. 6.6 Xbee Shield

Fig. 6.7 Ultrasonic Distance
Sensor Maxbotix LV-EZ1

- Hardware:
- 1 gigabyte (GB) of RAM
- 50 megabytes (MB) of available disk space for installation
- Software:
- Linux Operating System

- Database MySql 5.5
- JDK version 1.5 or higher
- Tomcat Server 6

Besides the aforementioned hardware components, the parking lot application uses a server computer responsible for hosting the SmartSensor PEM. The minimum configuration required for this computer to run the experiments is similar to the laptop computers. However, in a real installation this computer needs to be configured according to more specific systems requirements.

6.3 Application Development

The development of the application has three distinct phases. The first phase comprises the hardware configuration of the sensor nodes and the sink node. The second phase comprises the programming of the SIM components required to collect and interpret the signals collected by the WSN ultrasonic sensors. These components are to be installed at sensor nodes and sink nodes. The third phase is the programming and installation of the PEM mashup application built to monitor the parking lots registered in the SmartSensor infrastructure. To mount the ultrasonic sensors on the Arduino Uno boards, it is necessary to follow the following configuration steps (Fig. 6.8):

- To connect the sensor calibration pin to digital pin 13 of the Arduino board.
- To connect the sensor analog output to the Arduino analog pin 0.
- To connect the sensor voltage pin to the Arduino 5 V voltage pin.
- To connect the ground pin to the GND pin of the Arduino.

The configuration of the ultrasonic sensors of the experiment can be visualized in Fig. 6.9.

The first step to program the sensor nodes and configure the Gateway according to the application requirements is to assess the type of the required data delivery model. In general, the data delivery model of WSN applications can be of two kinds (or a combination of both): synchronous or asynchronous. In the synchronous model, network nodes must respond to an application request or should monitor some periodic event. To deal with synchronous events based on Request-Response operations, the SmartSensor provides developers with a REST Web service that is accessed through

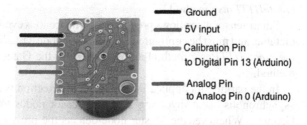

Fig. 6.8 Ultrasonic sensor setup

Ground

5V input

Calibration Pin
to Digital Pin 13 (Arduino)

Analog Pin
to Analog Pin 0 (Arduino)

Fig. 6.9 Ultrasonic sensor
mounted on the Arduino
board

the Gateway and returns the information collected by the sensor. The REST Web
service follows the following format:

```
http://{url_mis}/gateway/rest/getdata/{sensor}
```

To handle periodic events the developer must program the sensor node itself to
raise such events, i.e., the developer must set the parameters of sensing data rate and
sending data rate of the sensor node. For sensor nodes to send data to the gateway, the
developer must create an HTTP message using the *createHTTPmsg* method provided
by the SmartSensor HTTP library. This method has all the comprised elements of
an HTTP message: DHost, Shost, code, method, path, data and error. Where the
parameter "DHost" represents the id of the destination node, "Shost" the source node,
"code" represents the message type (for example, 2000 for discovery messages and 0
for sending data), "method" represents the HTTP verb (for example G for GET) and
"path" represents the type of sensor (for example, 5 for distance), "data" represents
the data collected by the sensor, and the parameter "error" sets the error value, if
any. To programming the sending of HTTP messages to the Gateway, the developer
uses the *sendHTTPmsg* method passing as a parameter a message created by the
createHTTPmsg method.

SmartSensor also allows processing asynchronous events. These events are unpre-
dictable, and must be configured on the sensor node, creating an HTTP message using
the *createHTTPmsg* method and sending it to the Gateway via the *sendHTTPmsg*
method.

In the parking lot application, the vehicle detection is programmed as a complex
asynchronous event involving a pair of sensor nodes (Master and Slave) and the
Gateway. Whenever the Master node detects the presence of an object it sends an

HTTP message to the Gateway informing the occurrence of the event. The Gateway, upon receiving of such message, makes a synchronous request to the Slave node to sense the current distance (object detection). After receiving the Slave response, the Gateway uses both measures to calculate the object size and determine if the detected object matches or not a vehicle. After a vehicle detection, the Gateway performs an update of the number of car parking spaces at the SIM database. This complex event is implemented by a component called "ParkingManager" that must be implemented by the application developer and installed at the Gateway node. The steps involved in the vehicle detection are illustrated in the UML sequence diagram of Fig. 6.10.

After the SIM programming and configuration, the next step in the programming of the parking lot Mashup application that will be installed in the SmartSensor PEM. This step starts with the building of a set of REST Web services that exposes information about the parking lot state. In the PoC application, we developed the following Web services:

- *ListParkingLots: This service provides a list of parking lots registered in infrastructure. The invocation of this service should follow the format:*

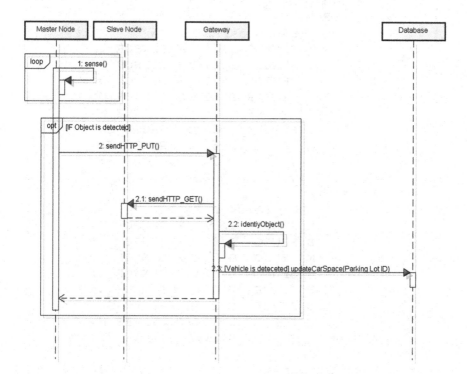

Fig. 6.10 Vehicle detection UML sequence diagram

`http://{PEM_SERVER}:8080/pem-v3.4-emml/ListSimEmml.`

Following an example of the XML file returned as response for this service:

```
▼<Results>
  ▼<Row>
    <LOCATION>R. Lobo Carneiro 470, Rio de Janeiro</LOCATION>
    <GATEWAY>146.164.247.208</GATEWAY>
    <LAST_ACCESS>2013-04-19 17:20:12.0</LAST_ACCESS>
    <FIRST_ACCESS>2013-04-19 15:48:12.0</FIRST_ACCESS>
  </Row>
</Results>
```

- getParkingLotInfo: This service provides the detailed information of a given parking lot registered in the infrastructure. The invocation of this service should follow the format: `http://{PEM_SVREER}:8080/pem-v3.4-emml/getParkingLotInfo? gatoway={url}`

where `url` is the address of the Gateway that manages the parking lot. The following code shows an example of the XML file returned as response for this service:

```
▼<Results>
  ▼<Row>
    <AREA_ID>1</AREA_ID>
    <M_SENSOR_I>51</M_SENSOR_I>
    <S_SENSOR_I>61</S_SENSOR_I>
    <M_SENSOR_O>71</M_SENSOR_O>
    <S_SENSOR_O>81</S_SENSOR_O>
    <T_SPACES_N>10</T_SPACES_N>
    <T_SPACES_S>2</T_SPACES_S>
    <C_SPACES_N>6</C_SPACES_N>
    <C_SPACES_S>1</C_SPACES_S>
  </Row>
  ▼<Row>
    <AREA_ID>2</AREA_ID>
    <M_SENSOR_I>52</M_SENSOR_I>
    <S_SENSOR_I>62</S_SENSOR_I>
    <M_SENSOR_O>72</M_SENSOR_O>
    <S_SENSOR_O>82</S_SENSOR_O>
    <T_SPACES_N>10</T_SPACES_N>
    <T_SPACES_S>2</T_SPACES_S>
    <C_SPACES_N>10</C_SPACES_N>
    <C_SPACES_S>2</C_SPACES_S>
  </Row>
</Results>
```

- getCarSpacesInfo: This service provides the historical information about car spaces of parking lots registered in the infrastructure. The invocation of this service should follow the format:

```
http://{PEM_SERVER}:8080/pem-v3.4-emml/gntCarSpacesInfo?gateway
={url},
```

where url is the address of the Gateway that manages the parking lot. The following code shows an example of the XML file returned as response for this service:

```
▼<Results>
  ▼<Row>
      <SPACE_ID>1</SPACE_ID>
      <AREA_ID>1</AREA_ID>
      <DATE>2013-03-22 16:00:35</DATE>
      <SPACE_TYPE>N</SPACE_TYPE>
      <IN_OUT>In</IN_OUT>
      <C_SPACES>9</C_SPACES>
  </Row>
  ▼<Row>
      <SPACE_ID>2</SPACE_ID>
      <AREA_ID>1</AREA_ID>
      <DATE>2013-03-22 16:01:02</DATE>
      <SPACE_TYPE>S</SPACE_TYPE>
      <IN_OUT>In</IN_OUT>
      <C_SPACES>1</C_SPACES>
  </Row>
  ▼<Row>
      <SPACE_ID>3</SPACE_ID>
      <AREA_ID>1</AREA_ID>
      <DATE>2013-03-22 16:01:45</DATE>
      <SPACE_TYPE>N</SPACE_TYPE>
      <IN_OUT>In</IN_OUT>
      <C_SPACES>8</C_SPACES>
  </Row>
  ▼<Row>
      <SPACE_ID>4</SPACE_ID>
      <AREA_ID>1</AREA_ID>
      <DATE>2013-03-22 16:01:45</DATE>
      <SPACE_TYPE>N</SPACE_TYPE>
      <IN_OUT>In</IN_OUT>
      <C_SPACES>7</C_SPACES>
  </Row>
  ▼<Row>
      <SPACE_ID>5</SPACE_ID>
      <AREA_ID>1</AREA_ID>
      <DATE>2013-03-22 16:01:45</DATE>
      <SPACE_TYPE>N</SPACE_TYPE>
      <IN_OUT>In</IN_OUT>
      <C_SPACES>6</C_SPACES>
  </Row>
</Results>
```

After the creation of the PEM services, the next step is to build the Web mashup application that integrate the information provided by the Web services and present

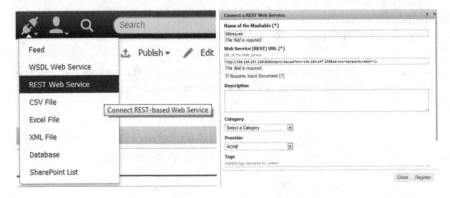

Fig. 6.11 Registering of PEM Web services within presto

this integrated view through a set of graphical user interfaces. Web Mashups can be built using any EMML editor. In this PoC we will show how to create Web Mashups using a popular graphical EMML editor and runtime environment called Presto [6].

First, it is necessary to integrate the PEM Web services created in the last step into the Presto platform. To do so, the Web services must be registered as data source for Mashup applications. This registration is done in the Presto platform through the instantiation of new REST Web Services connections, one for each Web service provided by PEM. Figure 6.11 illustrates the registration process within the Presto platform.

After registering all PEM Web services, we can start building the Web Mashup application. Figure 6.12 is a snapshot of the Presto graphical editor showing the specification of a data flow that processes the information generated by the get-CarSpacesInfo Web service, which is represented in the figure by the Presto *Mashable* object ParkingSpace. A *Mashable* object is any object that can be used as data source to create a Mashup application. The data flow specifies that the data received after the invocation of this service should be ordered using the object Sort and forwarded to the object Mashup Output.

Figure 6.13 illustrates the user interface that consumes the output of the EMML Mashup created in Fig. 6.12. This interface shows, in a tabular format and in real time, the entrance and exit of vehicles from a parking lot monitored by the PoC application.

The other functionalities of the PoC application are created using the same process. Figure 6.14 shows the user interface that displays the available car spaces in each lane of a parking lot. This application uses a PEM Web services that queries the database of the SIM responsible for monitoring the parking lot about the current state of its car spaces.

Finally, Fig. 6.15 illustrates the Web mashup application that integrates all the aforementioned user interface fragments into a unified view. The top of the window shows the number of car spaces available in each parking lot lane. At the bottom left is showed the entrance and exit of vehicles, on the right a map indicating the

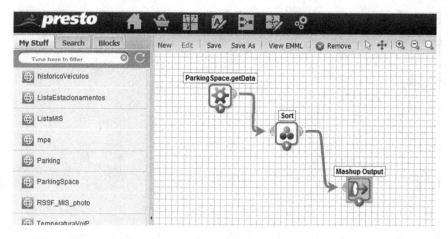

Fig. 6.12 Presto graphical editor

ParkingSpace					
Id ⇕	Corredor	Tipo De Vaga	Vagas Disponíveis	Data	Entrada/Saída
8	1	N	9	2013-03-22 16:04:55	Out
7	1	N	8	2013-03-22 16:04:46	Out
6	1	N	7	2013-03-22 16:04:30	Out
5	1	N	6	2013-03-22 16:01:45	In
4	1	N	7	2013-03-22 16:01:45	In
3	1	N	8	2013-03-22 16:01:45	In
2	1	S	1	2013-03-22 16:01:02	In
1	1	N	9	2013-03-22 16:00:35	In

Fig. 6.13 User interface for monitoring available car spaces

location of the parking lot, and at the bottom right a table shows general features of
the parking Lot, such as total car spaces by type, and current available spaces. Any
Web browser connected to the Internet can access this information.

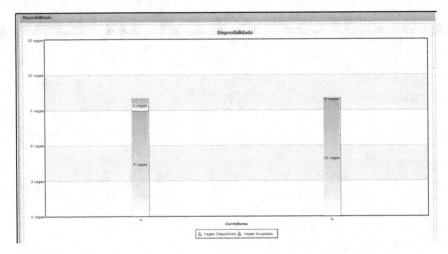

Fig. 6.14 User interface showing the available spaces in a parking lot

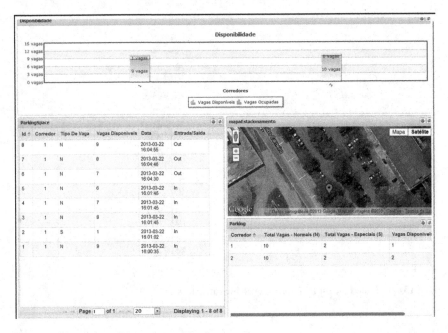

Fig. 6.15 Parking Lot Web mashup application

References

1. Liu, M., Mihaylov, S., Bao, Z., Jacob, M., Ives, Z., Loo, B., et al. (2010, September). SmartCIS: Integrating digital and physical environments. *SIGMOD Record, 39*, 48–53.
2. Nunes, R. J. C. (1995, November). *Integracão de Serviços para Edifcios Inteligentes.* (in Portuguese) PhD thesis, Instituto Superior Técnico, University of Lisbon, Lisbon, Portugal.
3. Chinrungrueng, J., Sunantachaikul, U., Triamlumlerd, S. (2007). Smart parking: An application of optical wireless sensor network. *Proceedings of the 2007 International Symposium on Applications and the Internet Workshops (SAINTW07).*
4. Vijay Kumar, P., Siddarth, T. S. (2010). A prototype parking system using wireless sensor networks. *International Joint Journal of Power, Control and Signal Processing (IJJCET2010), 1*(4), 78–82, www.ijjcet.com
5. Zigbee Protocol, http://www.sparkfun.com/datasheets/Wireless/Zigbee/XBee-Manual.pdf
6. Presto Platform, Retrieved May 2013, from http://prestocloud.jackbe.com/presto

Chapter 7
Final Remarks

Abstract In this chaper we summarize the contributions of this Book to advance the state-of-the-art in the development of IoT applications. The main contributions are: (i) to present a middleware-layer infrastructure, SmartSensor, that focuses on the integration of Wireless Sensor Networks (WSN) in the Web, providing WSN as a service, acessible as any other Web resource and enabling the discovery and composition of services to form Web mashup applications; (ii) to describe step by step the development of an application using the SmartSensor infrastructure, the Parking Lot Application, that helps drivers to find available parking space in a building. SmartSensor is composed of three software modules: (i) the Sensor Integration Module (SIM) integrates the distinct WSN devices and provides a RESTFUL interface to access them as Web resources; (ii) the Programming and Execution Module (PEM) enables the composition of value-added services from multiple Web sources; (iii) the Web 3.0 Integration Module (WIM) integrates the resources with Web 3.0 applications and platforms.

Keywords Internet of Things (IoT) · Web of Things (WoT) · Wireless sensor networks (WSN) · Middleware for IoT · SmartSensor · Parking lot application

7.1 Introduction

The Internet of Things (IoT) represents a new direction on the use of computers in everyday life as it enables the integration of the Internet with the physical world, populated with sensors, actuators, and embedded communication hardware. The heterogeneous physical devices become a part of the Web and can be accessible using the well-known Internet protocols. This scenario arises the opportunity for creating sophisticated applications based on physical world data, such as monitoring inaccessible and remote spaces (oil platforms, forests, tunnels, mines, pipes), environmental

F. C. Delicato et al., *Middleware Solutions for the Internet of Things,*   75
SpringerBriefs in Computer Science, DOI: 10.1007/978-1-4471-5481-5_7,
© The Author(s) 2013

monitoring (earthquakes, floods, radiation areas, fire, rainfall) [6], smart cities, smart buildings, smart homes, health-care, to name a few.

Some middleware platforms already exist, addressing one of the main challenges to enable realization of IoT: interoperability across heterogeneous resources to relieve the application developer from the burden of integrating them. However, according to [5], the existing proposals do not cover the full set of functionalities to meet the requirements of an IoT middleware. In addition, most of them are under development and did not reach the stage of maturity to be adopted in a large scale.

This Book described a middleware-layer infrastructure, SmartSensor, that focuses on the integration of Wireless Sensor Networks (WSN) in the Web, providing WSN as a service, acessible as any other Web resource and enabling the discovery and composition of services to form Web mashup applications. In fact, this infrastructure targets a significant barrier to the widespread use of WSNs, that is the complexity of applications development that need to deal with low-level concerns of WSN. One of the fundamental characteristic of SmartSensor is to be based on the REST (Representational State Transfer) principles [2] and to use Web standards and protocols, such as URIs (Uniform Resource Identifier) and HTTP (Hypertext Transfer Protocol). This is especially useful for the integration of WSN to the Web, since the heterogeneous nature of their devices. In SmartSensor, WSNs are connected to the Web through a gateway node and their data are exposed as RESTful Web resources. Therefore, the interactions occurs in a RESTFull style by using the set of simple, well-defined HTTP main operations (GET, POST, PUT and DELETE i.e. the verbs of REST). Currently, SmartSensor supports three different platforms that are proper to a WSN scenario typically endowed with several tiny and low-power networked devices in interaction.: Arduino,[1] Sun SPOT,[2] and motes from the MICA family (produced by MEMSIC, former Crossbow),[3] based on the TinyOS operating system,[4] specially designed to sensors.

The infrastructure provided by SmartSensor to seamless integrate the resources relies on three main building blocks:

1. The Sensor Integration Module (SIM) integrates the distinct WSN devices and provides a RESTfull interface to access them as Web resources. It enables data collection and delivery and supports publish and discovery of WSN services. SIM components are deployed both in sensor nodes and in gateways nodes.
2. The Programming and Execution Module (PEM) enables the composition of value-added services from multiple Web sources, mixing public available services and those provided by SmartSensor that are registered in SIMs. PEM offers a DSL (Domain Specific Language) based on the Enterpise Mashup Markup Language (EMML) [1] and an interpreter for such DSL. It provides mechanisms to create, interpret, and execute Web mashups specified via EMML scripts.

---

[1] http://www.arduino.cc/

[2] http://www.sunspotworld.com/

[3] http://www.memsic.com/

[4] http://www.tinyos.net/

3. The Web 3.0 Integration Module (WIM) integrates the resources with Web 3.0 applications and platforms.

This Book also detailed the development of a parking lot application that consists of a WSN-based vehicle detection system connected to the SmartSensor infrastructure. The three distinct phases involved in the development of such an application were discussed: (i) the hardware configuration of the sensor nodes and the sink node; (ii) the programming of the components to collect and interpret the signals collected by the WSN ultrasonic sensors; (iii) the programming and installation of the PEM mashup application to monitor the parking lots registered in the infrastructure. This application was used in three parking lots located at the Federal University of Rio de Janeiro (UFRJ).

7.2 Contributions

The main contributions of this work are:

- to present an overview on the emergent WoT paradigm, describing its main concepts, principles and building blocks;
- to describe a middleware-layer infrastructure that integrates distinct WSN endowed with a myriad of heterogeneous elements (sensors, actuators, communication hardware);
- to provide a RESTful-based programming model that hides, from the developer, the low-level details to integrate different types of WSN sensed data in a Mashup application. Using this programming model, developers can create applications without having specific knowledge about physical devices or networking environments;
- to describe, step by step, how to create a Web Mashup application using the Smart-Sensor infrastructure integrated with a widely used EMML graphical editor and runtime environment, Presto.[5] It is worthwhile to mention that SmartSensor can be used with any other tool based on EMML.

7.3 Future Work

Despite the rising popularity of IoT and the development of middleware solutions for facilitating the development of mashup applications, some important aspects need to be further addressed for making IoT a reality. The main functional components of an IoT middleware, stated by [5], includes interoperation, context detection, device discovery and management, security and privacy, and managing data volume. Although SmartSensor can be considered as a middleware for IoT, in its current version, it only

---

[5] http://www.jackbe.com/prestodocs/v3.2/presto-intro/prestoIntro.html

provides communication and integration services as well as a programming model
to develop applications on top of the WSN infrastructure.

Managing high data volume and supporting security and privacy are the two key
capabilities to be considered in next versions of SmartSensor. According to [6],
IoT generates a huge ammount of data, yielded by physical and virtual elements
connected to the Internet, and the data volume needs to be stored and easily reached.
The convergence of Cloud Computing with IoT has been pointed out as a promissing
approach [3] to address this issue by establish a cloud-based IoT environment, the
so-called *cloud-of-things* [4].

Another important issue that deserves a further investigation, highlighted by [7], is
the support for dynamic adaptation of mashups according to the user requirements and
the runtime environment. This aspect needs a combination of context monitoring and
management, adaptive behavior modeling, and the realization of dynamic adaptation
of the mashup.

References

1. Enterprise Mashup Markup Language, Open Mashup Alliance, 2010. Available at http://www.
   openmashup.org/
2. Fielding, R. (2000). *Architectural styles and the design of network-based software architectures*.
   Doctoral dissertation, University of California, Irvine.
3. Gao, L., Zhang, C., & Sun, L. (2011). *RESTful web of things API in sharing sensor data*. In the
   2011 International Conference on Internet Technology and Applications (iTAP), IEEE.
4. Soldatos, J., Serrano, M., & Hauswirth, M. (2012). Convergence of utility computing with the
   internet-of-things. *proceddings of the2012 Sixth International Conference on Innovative Mobile
   and Internet Services in Ubiquitous, Computing (IMIS'12)* (pp. 874–879).
5. Bandyopadhyay, S., Sengupta, M., Maiti, S., & Dutta, S. (2011). Role of middleware for internet
   of things: A study. *International Journal of Computer Science and Engineering Survey, 2*(3),
   94–105.
6. Vermesan, O., Friess, P., Guillermin, P., Gusmeroli, S., Sundmaeker, H., Bassi, A., Jubert,
   I., Mazura, M., Harrison, M., Eisenhauer, M., Doody, P. (2011). Internet of Things Strategic
   Research Roadmap. Global Technological and Societal Trends. (pp. 9–52). Aalborg: River Pub-
   lishers.
7. Zeng, D., Guo, S., & Cheng, Z. (2011). The web of things: A survey. *Journal of Communications,
   6*(6), 424–438. Sep 2011 doi:10.4304/jcm.6.6.424-438.